asy mediterranean

easy mediterranean

simple recipes from sunny shores

RYLAND
PETERS
& SMALL
LONDON NEW YORK

Editor Rachel Lawrence
Production Gemma Moules
Picture Research Emily Westlake
Publishing Director Alison Starling

Index Hilary Bird

First published in Great Britain in 2007.

This paperback edition published in 2009
by Ryland Peters & Small
20–21 Jockey's Fields
London WC1R 4BW
www.rylandpeters.com

10 9 8 7 6 5 4 3 2 1

Text © Maxine Clark, Clare Ferguson,
Silvana Franco, Brian Glover, Elsa Petersen-
Schepelern, Louise Pickford, Rena Salaman,
Jennie Shapter, Sonia Stevenson, Linda
Tubby, Fran Warde, and Ryland Peters &
Small 2007, 2009
Design and photographs
© Ryland Peters & Small 2007, 2009

Printed in China

ISBN: 978 1 84597 813 6

A CIP catalogue record for this book is
available from the British Library.

Notes

All spoon measurements are level unless
otherwise specified.

Ovens should be preheated to the specified
temperature. If using a convection oven,
cooking times should be reduced according
to the manufacturer's instructions.

Uncooked or partly cooked eggs should not
be served to the very young, the very old or
frail, or to pregnant women.

Speciality Asian ingredients are available in
larger supermarkets and Asian stores.

To sterilize preserving jars, wash them in hot,
soapy water and rinse in boiling water. Place
in a large saucepan and then cover with hot
water. With the saucepan lid on, bring the
water to a boil and continue boiling for
15 minutes. Turn off the heat, then leave the
jars in the hot water until just before they are
to be filled. Sterilize the lids for 5 minutes, by
boiling, or according to the manufacturer's
instructions. Jars should be filled and sealed
while they are still hot.

contents

mediterranean flavours

Famous for its sunshine, sandy shores and deep blue sea, the Mediterranean is also home to some of the most rich and varied cuisines in the world. From the seafood stews of southern France to the grilled meats of Greece and Turkey, every region has its own distinct dishes and ways of cooking.

Mediterranean cooking centres around exquisite fish and seafood, high-quality meats and a wealth of fruit, vegetables, pulses and grains. Thanks to the quality of the ingredients, many dishes are surprisingly easy to make – it's hard to beat a simple pasta dish made with the finest olive oil, juicy vine tomatoes and fragrant basil, for example. What's more, with its low saturated fat content and emphasis on fresh ingredients, it's healthy, too.

Food culture in this part of the world reflects the relaxed way of life that many Mediterraneans enjoy. Food and drink are things to be enjoyed at leisure and savoured. The tapas dishes of Spain and meze platters of Greece and Lebanon are a classic example of delicious little morsels designed to be enjoyed at a leisurely pace. At meal times, dishes are often served as separate courses, so that their flavours can be truly appreciated.

Whether you're planning on making a light lunch or a sumptuous feast, this book is packed with ideas and inspiration. With everything from starters and snacks to sweet things and drinks, there is something for everyone, including plenty of vegetarian options. So why not bring some sunshine into your kitchen and savour the flavours, aromas and colours of these mouthwatering recipes.

starters and snacks

chickpea fritters

Common in Sicily and North Africa, this ancient recipe is a marvellous, easy snack which can also be served with meat or fish. First it is cooked to a sort of thin porridge, which sets. Then it is cut up and cooked a second time, in olive oil, to a sweet crispness. A warning though – do not be tempted to change the order or you will find the mixture becomes lumpy and hard to manage. The fritters also make useful bases for canapés or as 'crisps' to serve with creamy dips.

Sieve the chickpea flour and salt together into a heavy-based saucepan. Whisk in 500 ml cold water until frothy and lump-free, then stir in the parsley. Bring to the boil, whisking constantly. About 2 minutes after it reaches the boil, it will suddenly thicken – take care as it may splatter.

Keep whisking over the heat for 1 more minute, then pour it out quickly into the oiled tray. Quickly smooth it flat with a spatula to just under 1 cm thickness before it begins to set, about 5–10 minutes.

Mark out into 12 squares, then make diagonal lines to give 24 triangles.

Put the olive oil in a frying pan or heavy-based saucepan and heat to 190°C (375°F). Add 6–8 triangles at a time and cook for 2 minutes on each side or until golden, blistered and crisp. Drain on crumpled kitchen paper. Serve hot or warm.

*Note Chickpea flour, also known as besan or gram flour, is sold in health food shops, delicatessens and Asian stores.

175 g chickpea flour*

1 teaspoon sea salt

a small bunch of fresh flat leaf parsley (about 30 g) chopped

250 ml extra virgin olive oil or olive oil, for frying

a metal tray, about 30 x 40 cm, oiled

MAKES 24

moroccan-style marinated black olives

750 g black olives in brine

2 tablespoons fennel or cumin seeds, crushed

1 tablespoon green cardamom pods, crushed

1 tablespoon small hot dried red chillies

2 tablespoons allspice berries, crushed

850 ml extra virgin olive oil

20-cm strip of orange zest, bruised

12 fresh bay leaves, washed, dried and bruised

1 large jar, 1.5 litres, sterilized, or 3 jars, 500 ml

MAKES 1.5 LITRES

Black olives, which have already been cured, will mellow even more if you crack them a little or prick with a fork, then marinate in aromatics and fine olive oil. Experiment, as many Moroccan householders do, until you find a flavour you like – your own customized blend.

Rinse the olives in cold water, drain, then pat dry with kitchen paper.

Put them on a clean dry surface such as a chopping board and crush them slightly with a meat hammer or rolling pin, or prick with a fork, to open up the flesh a little.

Put the fennel seeds, cardamom, chillies and allspice berries in a dry frying pan and toast over medium heat for a few minutes until aromatic.

Put the olive oil in a saucepan and heat to 180°C (350°F) – a cube of bread should turn golden-brown in 40–50 seconds. Let cool a little. Using a sterilized spoon, pack the orange zest, bay leaves, olives and spices into the jar in layers, until they all have been used. Cover with the hot olive oil. Let cool, uncovered. When cold, seal and store in a cool, dark place.

Leave for at least 1 week before tasting. These olives keep well and improve for some months.

This spicy Middle Eastern chickpea dip is deceptively easy to make. Dried chickpeas give a slightly nuttier flavour, but you can use canned chickpeas if you're in a hurry. It is delicious served as a dip with toasted pita breads or Chickpea Fritters (page 10). It also makes a great accompaniment to Falafels (page 20), kebabs or grilled chicken or meat.

hoummus

175 g dried chickpeas, soaked in cold water overnight, or 800 g canned chickpeas

2 tablespoons tahini paste

2 garlic cloves, chopped

freshly squeezed juice of 1–2 lemons

1 tablespoon ground cumin

2 tablespoons extra virgin olive oil

300 ml chickpea cooking liquid

sea salt and freshly ground black pepper

TO SERVE

1 tablespoon extra virgin olive oil

1 tablespoon fresh coriander, finely chopped

pita bread or triangles of toasted bread

SERVES 6

Drain and rinse the soaked chickpeas and put them in a saucepan. Cover with plenty of water, bring to the boil and skim until clear. Cover and cook until perfectly soft, about 1 hour. Alternatively, use a pressure cooker, following the manufacturer's instructions – cooking will take about 20 minutes.

Strain the chickpeas, reserving the cooking liquid. If using canned chickpeas, strain them first and discard the liquid, but use about 4 tablespoons cold water in the food processor.

If the tahini paste appears separated in the jar, mix it properly first. Divide all the ingredients into 2 batches and put the first batch in a food processor, then process briefly. Ideally it should still have some texture and should not be too solid. Taste and adjust the seasoning with salt and pepper and blend again briefly. Transfer to a bowl and repeat with the remaining ingredients.

Trickle a little oil over the top and sprinkle with the fresh coriander. Serve at room temperature with pita bread or triangles of toasted bread. In the summer, it is better served lightly chilled.

Aubergines are a key ingredient in many Mediterranean countries and can be cooked in a variety of ways. Some Middle Eastern cooks barbecue them to make babaghannouj, but in this recipe they are simply cut into cubes, coated in oil and roasted in the oven, which brings equally good results. This creamy dip can be served warm, cool or chilled as a starter or as part of a mixed meze.

babaghannouj

Toss the cubed aubergine in half the olive oil until coated. Arrange in a single layer in a shallow roasting tin or baking sheet and cook in a preheated oven at 200°C (400°F) Gas 6 for 20–25 minutes or until tender and slightly frizzled. Put the aubergine and its oil, the remaining olive oil, lemon juice, tahini paste, garlic, parsley and sea salt in a food processor. Blend for about 35–45 seconds to give a coarse but creamy paste. Taste and adjust the seasoning.

Serve warm, cool or chilled with an optional swirl of yoghurt or olive oil on top. Accompany with hot flatbreads or crisp fresh salad leaves.

*Note Tahina, tahine, tahini are variant spellings of the same thing. Though low-fat or less-toasted varieties do exist, you should avoid these. Always go for the full-flavoured type.

2 medium aubergines, about 500 g, cut into 2-cm cubes

125 ml extra virgin olive oil

4 tablespoons freshly squeezed lemon juice

4 tablespoons tahini paste*

3–4 garlic cloves, crushed

a bunch of fresh parsley, chopped

1 teaspoon sea salt flakes

plain yoghurt, to taste (optional)

flatbreads or salad leaves, to serve

SERVES 4–8

150 g whole shelled hazelnuts

100 g whole shelled almonds

100 g sesame seeds

75 g coriander seeds

50 g ground cumin

1 teaspoon sea salt

½ teaspoon freshly ground black pepper

TO SERVE

extra virgin olive oil

breadsticks or strips of toasted flatbread

MAKES ABOUT 500 g

No Egyptian home is complete without a jar of this wonderful seed and nut mixture in the larder. It is normally eaten as a snack – flatbreads are dipped first into olive oil, then into the dukkah. Breadsticks work well, too. Dukkah is also great used as a coating for chicken or fish instead of breadcrumbs.

egyptian dukkah

Put the hazelnuts, almonds and sesame seeds in an ovenproof dish in a preheated oven at 200°C (400°F) Gas 6 and toast for 5–10 minutes. Remove from the oven, then tip onto a plate to cool completely. If they aren't cool enough, they will turn oily when ground.

Toast the coriander seeds in a dry frying pan for 1–2 minutes until you can smell the aroma, tip onto the cooling nuts, then add the ground cumin to the pan. Toast for 30 seconds then transfer to the plate. When cold, put the nuts, spices, salt and pepper in a food processor and blend to a coarse, powdery meal – still dry-looking, but not totally pulverized. Spoon into a bowl and serve on a tray with a bowl of olive oil and the breadsticks.

falafels

These tasty broad bean patties are packed with fragrant herbs and spices. Falafels are a typical Lebanese street snack often served in pita breads with salad. They can also be served as a starter, with dips such as Hoummus (page 14), or as part of a more substantial meal with plain rice and a large bowl of refreshing Orange, Escarole and Black Olive Salad (page 62) or Greek Salad (page 66).

Drain and rinse the beans. Put them in a food processor, then add the onion, garlic, cumin, ground coriander, allspice, cayenne pepper and baking powder. Process to an almost-smooth paste.

Add the parsley and coriander and process briefly again. (You may have to divide the ingredients in half and process in 2 batches, depending on the size of your food processor.) Empty into a bowl and set aside for at least 1 hour.

Take 1 tablespoon of the mixture and shape it between your palms into a flat round shape, about 5-6 cm diameter. Repeat until all the mixture has been used.

Just before serving, heat 1 cm depth of oil in a large non-stick frying pan, add a single layer of the falafels and fry until golden and crisp on one side, then turn them over to crisp on the other side. Remove with a slotted spoon and drain on a plate lined with kitchen paper. Repeat until all the falafels have been fried. They are delicious served hot or at room temperature.

250 g dried, skinless broad beans, soaked overnight in cold water to cover

1 large onion, about 400 g, coarsely chopped

2 garlic cloves, crushed

1 tablespoon ground cumin

1 tablespoon ground coriander

1 teaspoon ground allspice

¼ teaspoon cayenne pepper

¼ teaspoon baking powder

200 g bunch of fresh parsley, coarsely chopped

a handful of fresh coriander, coarsely chopped

groundnut or sunflower oil, for deep-frying

MAKES ABOUT 20

RED PEPPER ROULADE

2 large red peppers

150 g mozzarella cheese

8 large fresh basil leaves

1 tablespoon Pesto alla Genovese (page 181)

extra virgin olive oil

sea salt and freshly ground black pepper

AUBERGINE, SALAMI AND ARTICHOKE

1 medium aubergine, about 200 g

6 tablespoons olive oil, plus extra for brushing

8 thin slices salami

4 artichokes marinated in oil, drained and halved

2 tablespoons freshly squeezed lemon juice

1 tablespoon capers, rinsed, drained and chopped

sea salt and freshly ground black pepper

LEMON-MARINATED COURGETTE

3 medium courgettes

4 tablespoons olive oil, plus extra for brushing

2 tablespoons freshly squeezed lemon juice

1 tablespoon freshly grated Parmesan cheese

2 anchovies, rinsed and finely chopped

cocktail sticks

a ridged stove-top grill pan

SERVES 4

Antipasti literally means 'before the meal' and are the delicious little first courses that traditionally begin an Italian meal. The best antipasti are an appealing mix of colours, flavours and textures, to whet the palate before the meal to come.

three marinated antipasti

To make the red pepper roulades, char-grill the peppers until soft and black. Rinse off the charred skin, cut the peppers in quarters lengthways, cut off the stalks and scrape out the seeds. Cut the mozzarella into 8 thin slices. Put a slice inside each pepper strip, put a basil leaf on top and season well with salt and pepper. Roll up from one end and secure with a cocktail stick. Put the pesto in a bowl and beat in enough olive oil to thin it to pouring consistency. Add the rolls and toss to coat. Cover and let marinate for at least 2 hours.

To make the aubergine antipasto, heat a ridged stove-top grill pan until hot. Cut the aubergine into 8 thin slices, brush lightly with olive oil and cook for 2–3 minutes on each side. Put a slice of salami on each one, then a halved artichoke at one side. Fold the aubergine in half to cover the artichoke, secure with a cocktail stick and put in a shallow dish. Put the 6 tablespoons olive oil in a bowl, whisk in the lemon juice, capers, salt and pepper, then spoon over the aubergines. Cover and let marinate as above.

To make the lemon-marinated courgette, cut the courgettes into long, thin slices, brush with olive oil and cook on the same grill pan for 2–3 minutes on each side. Transfer to a shallow dish. Beat the olive oil, lemon juice, Parmesan and anchovies together in a bowl, then pour over the courgettes. Cover and let marinate as above. Serve all three as mixed antipasti.

slow-roasted tomatoes on bruschetta with salted ricotta

8 large, ripe plum or round tomatoes

2 garlic cloves, finely chopped

1 tablespoon dried oregano

4 tablespoons extra virgin olive oil

50 g salted ricotta or feta cheese, thinly sliced

sea salt and freshly ground black pepper

basil leaves, to serve (optional)

BRUSCHETTA

4 thick slices country bread, preferably sourdough

2 garlic cloves, halved

extra virgin olive oil, for drizzling

SERVES 4

These firm but juicy roasted tomatoes burst with the flavour of the sun. They take no time to prepare but a long time concentrating their flavours in the oven – they smell fantastic while cooking! Plum tomatoes have less moisture in them and work well. You can use other vine-ripened varieties – just make sure they have some taste!

If using plum tomatoes cut them in half lengthways; if using round ones cut them in half crossways. Put them cut side up on a baking sheet. Mix the garlic and oregano with the olive oil, and season with salt and pepper. Spoon or brush this mixture over the cut tomatoes. Bake in a preheated oven at 170°C (325°F) Gas 3 for about 2 hours, checking them occasionally. They should be slightly shrunk and still a brilliant red colour. If they are too dark they will be bitter. Let cool.

To make the bruschetta, grill, toast or pan-grill the bread on both sides until lightly charred or toasted. Cut the bruschetta slices to size so that 2 tomato halves will sit on top of each one. Rub the top side of each slice with the cut garlic, then drizzle with olive oil.

Put 2 tomato halves on each bruschetta, sprinkle with the slivered cheese and top with a basil leaf, if liked. Serve at room temperature.

1 Italian sfilatino or thin French baguette, sliced into thin rounds

extra virgin olive oil, for brushing

TAPENADE

175 g Greek-style black olives, such as Kalamata, pitted

2 garlic cloves

3 canned anchovies, drained

2 teaspoons capers, drained

1 tablespoon extra virgin olive oil, plus extra to cover

WHITE BEAN PURÉE

2 tablespoons olive oil

2 garlic cloves, finely chopped

1 teaspoon very finely chopped fresh rosemary

1 small red chilli, deseeded and finely chopped

400 g canned cannellini beans, rinsed and drained

sea salt and freshly ground black pepper

TO SERVE

chopped fresh parsley

SERVES 6–8

The combination of bland creamy beans and sharp, rich, salty tapenade makes a sublime mouthful, especially when spread on crisp crostini. You can use any type of canned bean for this, but the whiter they are the prettier they look. If you like, chop up some more black olives and sprinkle them on the bean purée or crumble some crisply cooked bacon over the top for extra crunch.

white bean and black olive crostini

To make the tapenade, put the olives, garlic, anchovies, capers and olive oil into a food processor and blend until smooth. Scrape out into a jar, cover with a layer of olive oil and set aside.

Brush both sides of each slice of bread with olive oil and spread out on a baking sheet. Bake in a preheated oven at 190°C (375°F) Gas 5 about 10 minutes until crisp and golden.

Meanwhile, make the white bean purée. Heat the oil in a small frying pan and add the garlic. Cook gently for 2 minutes until golden but not browned. Stir in the rosemary and chilli. Remove from the heat, add the beans and 3 tablespoons water. Mash the beans roughly with a fork and return to the heat until warmed through. Taste and season with salt and pepper.

Spread a layer of tapenade on the crostini followed by a spoonful of bean purée. Scatter with parsley and serve immediately.

caponata

Caponata is similar to ratatouille, but much more exotic. There are dozens of variations of this delectable dish from Sicily, which is usually served as a starter at room temperature. It improves with age, so make a big batch and keep in the refrigerator.

Sprinkle the aubergine with the salt, toss well and let stand for 10 minutes. Drain and pat dry with kitchen paper.

Put the olive oil into a large, heavy-based saucepan and heat until very hot. Add the onion, garlic, olives and capers. Stir over high heat for 2–3 minutes, then add the aubergine and continue to cook, stirring, over medium heat for another 8 minutes. Using a slotted spoon, transfer the mixture to a plate and set aside.

Add the oregano, marjoram or thyme to the pan, then add the tomatoes, courgettes, tomato purée, sugar and stock or water. Stir gently and bring to the boil. Reduce the heat and simmer for 8 minutes. Return the aubergine mixture to the pan and simmer gently until the flavours have mingled. The vegetables should still be intact, not mushy.

Dip the pan into a bowl of cold water to cool.

To serve, transfer to a bowl, sprinkle with parsley and top with the extra sprigs of oregano, marjoram or thyme, if using. Caponata may be served warm, cool or cold, but not chilled.

1 aubergine, about 300 g, cut into 1-cm cubes

1 tablespoon salt

4 tablespoons extra virgin olive oil

2 red onions, cut into 8 wedges each

4 garlic cloves, chopped

100 g dry-cured green olives

75 g dry-cured black olives

50 g capers in salt

2 teaspoons freshly chopped oregano, marjoram or thyme leaves, plus extra sprigs, to serve (optional)

3 tomatoes, about 300 g, cut into 8 wedges each

2 baby courgettes, about 200 g, sliced crossways

2 tablespoons tomato purée

2 teaspoons sugar

150 ml chicken or vegetable stock or water

4 tablespoons chopped fresh flat leaf parsley

SERVES 6–8

There are many versions of this recipe, but when served as a meze dish, the stuffing is usually a simple, aromatic mixture of rice, onions and herbs. They are time consuming to make, but invite your friends around and enlist some help; the results are well worth the effort. Serve with other meze dishes, such as Moroccan-style Marinated Black Olives, Falafels (page 20) and Spicy Meat Pastries (page 38).

stuffed vine leaves

Bring a large saucepan of water to the boil and blanch the fresh vine leaves for 1–2 minutes in batches of 5–6 at a time. Remove with a slotted spoon and drain in a colander. They should just be wilted. If using preserved leaves, remember they are very salty – rinse first, then soak in a bowl of hot water for 3–5 minutes. Remove, rinse again and drain in a colander.

To make the stuffing, put half the lemon juice in a large bowl. Add the rice, onions, spring onions, dill, mint, parsley, olive oil, salt and pepper and stir well.

Line the base of a wide saucepan with 4 or 5 vine leaves. Place a vine leaf, rough side up, on a chopping board (handle the leaves carefully as they are fragile). Put a heaped teaspoon of the stuffing near the stalk end, fold the 2 opposite sides over the stuffing and roll up tightly like a fat cigar. Repeat with the remaining leaves.

Arrange the stuffed vine leaves in tight circles in the saucepan with the loose ends underneath. Pour the olive oil and the remaining lemon juice over the top and set a small inverted plate on top to stop them opening up while cooking. Add the measured hot water, cover and simmer gently for 50 minutes.

Serve hot or at room temperature on a platter lined with fresh vine leaves, if available.

55 fresh vine leaves, plus extra to serve (optional), or 225 g preserved vine leaves

4 tablespoons extra virgin olive oil

450 ml hot water

STUFFING

freshly squeezed juice of 1 lemon, strained

150 g long grain rice, rinsed

2 large onions, finely chopped (not grated)

5 spring onions, including white parts, trimmed and thinly sliced

4 tablespoons fresh dill, finely chopped

2 tablespoons fresh mint, finely chopped

2 tablespoons finely chopped fresh flat leaf parsley

5 tablespoons extra virgin olive oil

sea salt and freshly ground black pepper

MAKES 50

48 small uncooked prawns, about 600 g, shelled and deveined, with tail shell left on

4 tablespoons extra virgin olive oil

8 garlic cloves, bruised

6 small dried chillies

8 small fresh bay leaves

freshly squeezed juice of ½ lemon

sea salt

ALIOLI

5 garlic cloves, finely chopped

a large pinch of salt

100 ml extra virgin olive oil

2 teaspoons freshly squeezed lemon juice, plus extra to taste

100 ml sunflower oil

fine sea salt and freshly ground white pepper

4 individual cazuelas (terracotta ramekins), 10-12 cm diameter, preheated in a hot oven

SERVES 4

This mouthwatering dish is a staple on many tapas menus in Spain. It is traditionally served sizzling hot in individual terracotta bowls called cazuelas, accompanied by a small bowl of alioli (garlic mayonnaise). Tapas are little dishes designed to accompany pre-dinner drinks, such as a glass of wine or chilled fino sherry.

garlic prawns

To make the alioli, pound the garlic and a large pinch of salt to a smooth, thick, creamy consistency with a mortar and pestle. Slowly drip in the olive oil, mixing with the pestle. Switch to a whisk and mix in the lemon juice, white pepper and, little by little, half the sunflower oil. Add 1–2 teaspoons cold water and whisk well while adding the remaining oil. The mixture will be very thick. Set aside for at least 30 minutes for the garlic to mellow, then add salt, pepper and extra lemon juice to taste.

To prepare the prawns, put them on a plate and sprinkle lightly with salt. Heat the olive oil in a frying pan, add the garlic and fry until brown. Add the chillies, bay leaves and prawns all at once and fry without turning until the prawns are crusted and curled on one side, then turn them over and crust the other side, about 3½ minutes in total.

Transfer to the preheated cazuelas, sprinkle with lemon juice and top with a spoonful of alioli. Serve immediately while still bubbling hot.

clams with chilli parsley sauce

1 kg small clams, scrubbed, rinsed and drained

4 tablespoons extra virgin olive oil

1 teaspoon dried chilli flakes

4 garlic cloves, chopped

1 onion, finely chopped

125 ml dry or sweet white vermouth

freshly ground black pepper

a handful of fresh parsley, chopped, plus 4–6 leaves, to serve (optional)

SERVES 4–6

Clam dishes in Italy are wonderful and this sweet shellfish is used in many different ways, all simple and delicious. Serve this as a starter with toasted ciabatta to mop up the sauce. Another classic dish is Pasta con le Vongole (page 187) – pasta with clam sauce.

Put the clams, olive oil, chilli flakes, garlic, onion, vermouth and black pepper into a large saucepan. Bring to the boil, cover tightly with a lid, reduce the heat and let steam for about 4–6 minutes.

Stir in the chopped parsley and cover again. Turn off the heat, let steam for a further 1 minute, then serve, topped with a parsley leaf, if using.

Note Canned or bottled clams in the shell are widely available in Italian delis and are useful if you can't find any fresh clams. If using canned or bottled clams, drain the liquid into the pan, add all the remaining ingredients except the clams, bring to the boil and reduce to about 250 ml. Add the drained clams, then steam just until the clams have been heated through. Serve as above.

250 g piece of sashimi-grade tuna or swordfish or swordfish loin (thin end)

125 g rocket

freshly shaved Parmesan cheese

DRESSING

freshly squeezed juice of 3 lemons

150 ml extra virgin olive oil

1 garlic clove, finely chopped

1 tablespoon salted capers, rinsed and chopped

a pinch of dried chilli flakes

sea salt and freshly ground black pepper

SERVES 4

This dish requires good-quality sashimi-grade tuna or swordfish, which a good fishmongers should be able to provide. Chilling or lightly freezing it makes it firm enough to slice very thinly. As soon as the slices hit plates at room temperature, they become meltingly soft.

fresh tuna carpaccio

Trim the tuna of any membrane or gristle. Wrap tightly in clingfilm and freeze for about 1 hour, until just frozen but not rock solid.

Meanwhile, to make the dressing, put the lemon juice, olive oil, garlic, capers, chilli flakes, salt and pepper in a bowl and whisk until emulsified.

Unwrap the tuna and slice it thinly with a sharp, thin-bladed knife. Arrange the slices so they completely cover 4 large dinner plates. Spoon the dressing over the top. Add a tangle of rocket and sprinkle with Parmesan shavings, then serve.

175 g plain flour

½ teaspoon sea salt

2 tablespoons extra virgin olive oil

1 egg yolk, lightly beaten

FILLING

3–4 tablespoons extra virgin olive oil

1 large onion, finely chopped

200 g lean minced lamb

1 teaspoon ground allspice

1 teaspoon ground cumin

a large pinch of ground cinnamon

freshly squeezed juice of 1 lemon

3 tablespoons raisins, rinsed

150 ml hot water

3 tablespoons finely chopped fresh mint leaves

2 tablespoons pine nuts, toasted in a dry frying pan

sea salt and freshly ground black pepper

a round 8-cm pastry cutter

MAKES ABOUT 30

Packed with sweet and sour flavours, these intricate little pastries are known as sambusak in Greece where they are often served as part of a mixed meze. Traditionally fried, they can also be baked.

spicy meat pastries

To make the pastry, sift the flour and salt into a bowl. Make a well in the centre, add the olive oil and mix with your fingers. Add 90 ml water and knead until a soft, neat ball is formed. Cover with clingfilm and let rest for 30 minutes.

To make the filling, heat the olive oil in a saucepan, add the onion and sauté until it turns light brown, about 10 minutes. Increase the heat and add the lamb, turning and breaking up the lumps until all the moisture has evaporated and it starts to sizzle. Add the allspice, cumin, cinnamon, salt and pepper and brown for 2–3 minutes. Add the lemon juice, raisins and the hot water, then cover and cook for 20 minutes. It should be a fairly dry mixture by then. Add the mint and pine nuts and set aside.

Divide the pastry in half. Put one piece on a lightly-floured surface and roll out thinly to a circle about 30 cm in diameter, turning the pastry frequently. Cut out rounds with the pastry cutter. Gather the remaining pastry from around the discs and add it to the remaining portion of pastry. Knead until soft again, cover and set aside.

Have a small bowl of cold water by you. Put 1 teaspoon of filling in the middle of a round of pastry. Dip a finger in the water and wet the edges, then fold half of the pastry over the other half making a half-moon shape. Press the edges firmly to seal and put it on an oiled baking sheet. Repeat until all the rounds have been used. Roll out the remaining pastry, cut out more rounds and repeat the process.

Brush the tops with the egg yolk and bake in a preheated oven at 200°C (400°F) Gas 6 for 10–12 minutes until light golden.

Tapas bars, or tascas, are found all over Spain and serve an impressive range of little dishes to accompany a glass of sherry or wine. The word tapa means lid and originally referred to a slice of bread placed on top of a glass to keep the flies away. These delectable fritters should be served very hot, with lots of napkins, cocktail sticks and a bowl of coarse sea salt.

potato fritters with chorizo

Boil the potatoes in a saucepan of salted water until soft, drain through a colander and cover with a cloth for about 5 minutes to let them dry out. Transfer to a bowl, mash in the flour and season with a little black pepper. Mix in the egg yolks, then stir in the chorizo.

Put the egg whites in a separate bowl and whisk until soft peaks form. Fold into the mashed potatoes a little at a time.

Fill a saucepan or deep-fryer one-third full with oil, or to the manufacturer's recommended level. Heat to 180°C (350°F).

Working in batches of 6, take heaped teaspoons of the mixture and lower into the hot oil. Fry each batch for 3 minutes until evenly golden, turning them over halfway through (if they brown too quickly they will not have a good texture in the centre). Keep the oil temperature constant. As each batch is done, drain on kitchen paper and keep them warm in a preheated oven 180°C (350°F) Gas 4 until all have been cooked. Serve hot.

500 g potatoes, peeled and cut lengthways into thick fingers

1 tablespoon self-raising flour

2 large eggs, separated, plus 1 egg white

100 g chorizo, skinned and chopped into small pieces

sea salt and freshly ground black pepper

olive or sunflower oil, for deep-frying

MAKES ABOUT 24

bresaola and rocket
with olive oil and parmesan

Bresaola is Italian cured, air-dried beef – flavourful, deep crimson, lean and succulent. Preferably it should be cut from the piece, sliced very thinly, but it is also available pre-sliced, in packs. This combination of mellow, salty meat with the sharp, savoury taste of Parmesan and best quality extra virgin olive oil is simple, but wonderful.

12–16 thin slices of bresaola

50 g Parmesan cheese, in the piece

a large handful of wild rocket

4–6 teaspoons extra virgin olive oil

SERVES 4

Arrange the slices of bresaola on 4 serving plates.

Using a vegetable peeler or sharp knife, shave off thin curls of the Parmesan and drop them on top of the bresaola.

Scatter the rocket over the top, then drizzle with the olive oil. Serve immediately.

Tapas bars, or tascas, are found all over Spain and serve an impressive range of little dishes to accompany a glass of sherry or wine. The word tapa means lid and originally referred to a slice of bread placed on top of a glass to keep the flies away. These delectable fritters should be served very hot, with lots of napkins, cocktail sticks and a bowl of coarse sea salt.

potato fritters with chorizo

Boil the potatoes in a saucepan of salted water until soft, drain through a colander and cover with a cloth for about 5 minutes to let them dry out. Transfer to a bowl, mash in the flour and season with a little black pepper. Mix in the egg yolks, then stir in the chorizo.

Put the egg whites in a separate bowl and whisk until soft peaks form. Fold into the mashed potatoes a little at a time.

Fill a saucepan or deep-fryer one-third full with oil, or to the manufacturer's recommended level. Heat to 180°C (350°F).

Working in batches of 6, take heaped teaspoons of the mixture and lower into the hot oil. Fry each batch for 3 minutes until evenly golden, turning them over halfway through (if they brown too quickly they will not have a good texture in the centre). Keep the oil temperature constant. As each batch is done, drain on kitchen paper and keep them warm in a preheated oven 180°C (350°F) Gas 4 until all have been cooked. Serve hot.

500 g potatoes, peeled and cut lengthways into thick fingers

1 tablespoon self-raising flour

2 large eggs, separated, plus 1 egg white

100 g chorizo, skinned and chopped into small pieces

sea salt and freshly ground black pepper

olive or sunflower oil, for deep-frying

MAKES ABOUT 24

4 tablespoons extra virgin olive oil

1 Spanish onion, sliced into rings

3 garlic cloves, sliced

2 red peppers, halved, deseeded and sliced

2 yellow peppers, halved, deseeded and sliced

2 ripe red tomatoes, skinned and sliced

6 eggs

4 slices jamon Serrano ham or Parma ham

1 dried red chilli, crumbled (optional)

sea salt and freshly ground black pepper

SERVES 6–8

Versions of this handsome, delicious dish are found all over Spain, the Basque country and the South of France. Geographical origins will dictate the exact ingredients and treatment – but peppers, garlic, tomatoes, ham and often eggs are essentials, as is fruity, robust olive oil. Try crumbling in some dried chillies for a spicier version.

piperrada

Heat 3 tablespoons of the oil in a heavy-based frying pan over a medium heat. Add the onions and garlic and sauté until soft and fragrant but not browned. Add the peppers and tomatoes. Cover the pan, reduce the heat and cook to form a soft thick purée, about 8–12 minutes. Season to taste.

Break the eggs into a bowl, add salt and pepper and stir with a fork. Using a spatula, push a space clear near the centre of the pan. Add the remaining oil to the space, then pour in the eggs. Stir gently over medium heat until semi-set. Turn off the heat.

Fold the slices of ham into rosettes or pleats, then add to the pan. Crumble over some hot chilli, if using, and serve straight from the pan.

Note Rounds or triangles of bread fried in olive oil are often served as an accompaniment to piperrada.

char-grilled pepper frittata

1 small red pepper,
quartered and deseeded

1 small yellow pepper,
quartered and deseeded

1 small green pepper,
quartered and deseeded

2 tablespoons ricotta or
mascarpone cheese

6 large eggs

2 tablespoons fresh thyme leaves

2 tablespoons extra virgin olive
or sunflower oil

1 large red onion, sliced

1 tablespoon balsamic vinegar

2 garlic cloves, crushed

sea salt and freshly
ground black pepper

*a 20-cm heavy frying pan
(measure the base, not the top)*

SERVES 2–3

A frittata should be cooked slowly and be only lightly coloured and still slightly moist when served. The Italians usually flip them to finish cooking, but often a recipe will suggest quickly flashing the frittata under the grill or putting it in a hot oven just to set the top. They can also be cut into squares and served cold, if desired.

Put the peppers skin side up under a preheated grill and cook until the skins have charred. Transfer to a bowl, cover and let cool. This will steam off the skins, making them easier to remove.

Put the cheese in a large bowl, add 1 egg and mix to loosen the cheese. Whisk in the remaining eggs with a fork. Season with salt, pepper and thyme and stir into the cheese mixture.

Peel the charred skins off the peppers and rinse under cold running water. Pat dry with kitchen paper and cut into thick strips. Stir into the bowl.

Heat half the oil in the frying pan, add the sliced onion and balsamic vinegar and cook over gentle heat for about 10 minutes until softened. Add the garlic and cook for 1 minute.

Using a slotted spoon, add the onion to the egg mixture and stir. Add the remaining oil to the pan and heat gently. Pour the frittata mixture into the pan and let cook over low heat until almost set, puffy and light golden-brown on the underside.

Finish under a preheated grill or put a plate or flat saucepan lid on top of the pan and invert the pan so the frittata drops onto the plate or lid. Slide back into the pan and cook for 30–60 seconds. Transfer to a serving plate and serve hot or at room temperature, cut into wedges.

soups and salads

There are numerous variations of this chilled, tomato-based soup from Spain. Originally, it was a peasant dish that made use of the three basic ingredients much revered in Spain – oil, water and bread and other ingredients were added according to what was available. If you chill it, put it in a container with a tight-fitting lid so the flavours don't mingle with anything else in the refrigerator.

gazpacho

Put ¼ of the chopped onion in a small bowl and add ¼ teaspoon of the sugar, ½ teaspoon of the vinegar, and 3 tablespoons cold water and set aside. Reserve one-quarter of the prepared red and green peppers and put in small bowls. These small bowls will be served as garnishes at the end.

To make the other garnishes, put the unpeeled, chopped cucumber, croutons, and chopped tomatoes in separate small bowls and set aside.

To make the gazpacho, put the bread, garlic, and remaining sugar in a flat dish, sprinkle with the remaining vinegar and 250 ml cold water, and let soak.

Cut the skinned tomatoes in half and cut out the hard core. Put a sieve over a bowl and deseed the tomatoes into the sieve. Push the seeds with a ladle to extract all the juices. Put the juices in a blender and discard the seeds. Add the soaked bread mixture and half the tomatoes. Blend until smooth and pour into a bowl.

Put the remaining tomatoes, the remaining onion, and 100 ml iced water in the blender. Pulse 8 times to get a medium chunky effect, then pour into the bowl. Put the remaining chopped peppers, coarsely chopped cucumber, olive oil, salt and 150 ml iced water in the blender and pulse 8 times. Add to the bowl and stir in Tabasco, if using. Chill for up to 2 hours.

If you like ice added, serve with crushed ice cubes. Put the bowls of garnishes on the table for guests to sprinkle over the gazpacho.

1 large sweet Spanish onion, finely chopped

1½ teaspoons sugar

4 tablespoons white wine vinegar

1 large red pepper, peeled with a vegetable peeler and coarsely chopped

1 large green pepper, peeled with a vegetable peeler and coarsely chopped

3 slices country-style bread, with crusts, about 100 g

3 garlic cloves, crushed

2.5 kg ripe tomatoes, skinned

12 cm cucumber, peeled and coarsely chopped

6 tablespoons extra virgin olive oil

fine sea salt

a splash of Tabasco (optional)

ice (optional)

GARNISHES

6 cm cucumber, unpeeled, finely chopped

1 cm bread croutons, sautéed in olive oil infused with garlic

2 ripe tomatoes, finely chopped

SERVES 6

750 g asparagus

3 tablespoons extra virgin olive oil

1 tablespoon butter

2 leeks, well washed and thinly sliced

1 onion, finely chopped

1 litre chicken stock

freshly grated nutmeg

150 ml double cream

sea salt and freshly ground white pepper

a mouli (optional)

SERVES 4

Asparagus is regarded as a delicacy in many parts of France and Spain and is often simply steamed and served with a vinaigrette for dipping. This delicious, creamy soup is another wonderful way to cook and eat it.

cream of asparagus soup

Cut the tips off 8 asparagus spears and reserve. Chop the rest into 2-cm pieces.

Heat the olive oil and butter in a saucepan, add the leeks and onion, cover and sauté over gentle heat for 10 minutes. Add the chopped asparagus, stock and a pinch of nutmeg, season well with salt and pepper and simmer for 10 minutes.

Transfer to a blender, purée until smooth, then, using the back of a ladle, push through a sieve set over a bowl. Alternatively, use a mouli. Add two-thirds of the cream to the bowl and stir well. Return the soup to the saucepan and heat gently when ready to serve (do not let boil).

Cook the reserved asparagus tips in boiling water until just tender. Ladle the soup into bowls, spoon the remaining cream on top, add the asparagus tips and another pinch of nutmeg, then serve.

soupe au pistou

Pistou is the Provençal version of Italian pesto, and to make it you need a big bunch of fresh basil. This version of the soup is quicker to cook than the traditional one and can be made with your choice of Mediterranean vegetables.

To make the pistou, put the basil and garlic in a food processor and blend as finely as possible. Add enough olive oil in a steady stream to form a loose paste. Set aside.

Heat the measured olive oil in a small frying pan, add the onion wedges and fry gently on both sides until softened. Cook the potato and soup pasta in boiling salted water until tender. Drain. Blanch the carrots, Brussels sprouts, pepper and peas in boiling salted water until tender but crisp, about 3–5 minutes. Drain and refresh in cold water.

Bring the stock to the boil and add salt and pepper, the pasta, vegetables and cannellini beans. Simmer for 2 minutes or until heated through.

Serve in heated soup plates, with a separate bowl of pistou for guests to stir into their soup.

4 tablespoons extra virgin olive oil

1 red onion, cut into wedges

1 large potato, cut into 1-cm cubes

a handful (about 125 g) of soup pasta, such as orecchiette (or the traditional vermicelli)

4 baby carrots, halved or quartered lengthways

250 g Brussels sprouts, halved, or baby courgettes, cut into thick slices

1 red pepper, halved, deseeded and sliced

250 g shelled green peas

1 litre chicken or vegetable stock

250 g cooked cannellini beans, rinsed and drained

sea salt and freshly ground black pepper

PISTOU

leaves from 1 large bunch of basil

2 garlic cloves, crushed

olive oil

SERVES 4

avgolemono

250 ml long grain rice

1½ litres chicken or
vegetable stock

2 large eggs

grated zest and freshly
squeezed juice of
2 large lemons

sea salt and freshly ground
white pepper

TO SERVE

a large handful of fresh flat leaf
parsley, finely chopped

1 small lemon, thinly sliced
(optional)

SERVES 4

The name of this classic Greek soup literally means 'egg-lemon'. It is incredibly fresh and very easy to prepare. If you're serving it to guests, prepare the stock and rice first, then complete the dish just before serving.

Wash the rice well to remove the starch, then drain in a sieve.

Put the stock in a large saucepan and bring to the boil. Add the rinsed rice and return to the boil. Reduce to a simmer and cook for about 20 minutes or until the rice is tender. Season with salt and pepper.

Put the eggs in a small bowl and whisk well. Stir in the lemon juice and 1 tablespoon water.

Remove the soup from the heat and whisk one ladle of soup into the egg mixture. Add 2 more ladles, whisking again. Return the egg mixture to the pan and stir well.

Serve the soup in wide, shallow bowls, with a sprinkling of parsley and a little lemon zest. Float a few paper-thin slices of lemon on top if you like.

Note Do not reboil the soup after adding the eggs, or they will scramble.

This superb, ancient recipe from Provence excites huge passion and interest. Bouillabaisse consists of fragrant fish chunks poached in a saffron-enhanced broth. The dish is served as two courses: first the broth is spooned over toasted bread croûtes topped with rouille (rust) sauce, which enriches the soup; next the fish itself is eaten. It is undoubtedly a triumph, so do devote several hours to making it.

bouillabaisse

To make the aïoli, put the garlic, salt, egg and egg yolks in a food processor and blend until creamy. Gradually pour in the olive oil until the mixture is thick and emulsified. Add the lemon juice and blend briefly to combine. Set aside.

Heat half the olive oil in a large, flameproof casserole, add the onions, leeks, garlic and tomatoes and sauté until golden and wilted. Add the thyme, fennel and orange zest. Add the boiling water and the remaining oil, then add the fish and shellfish (except the mussels or clams) and half the saffron.

Return to the boil, reduce the heat and simmer for 10–12 minutes or until the fish is opaque. Add the mussels and clams, if using, and cook for 3–4 minutes until they open. Discard any that don't.

Pour the pan contents through a colander into a large bowl. Lift out the fish into a large, heated tureen or serving dish. Using a slotted spoon, press down on the onions, fennel, thyme and tomatoes in the colander, then discard them.

Pour the broth back into the rinsed pan, bring to the boil and cook over very high heat for 5 minutes until emulsified, then whisk in half the aïoli. Add the hot potatoes and stir in the Pernod, if using. Pour about a quarter of the mixture over the fish.

Put a croûte on the side of each soup bowl, then add a generous spoonful of aïoli to each. Mix the remaining aïoli with the harissa and remaining saffron to create a scarlet rouille sauce. Add a spoonful of rouille to the croûtes. Ladle hot soup into each dish.

When the soup is finished, serve the fish and hot potatoes with any remaining aïoli and rouille.

50 ml extra virgin olive oil

2 large onions, quartered

2 leeks, cut into 5-cm chunks

4 garlic cloves, chopped

2 large red tomatoes, skinned, quartered and deseeded

a bunch of fresh thyme, about 50 g

1 fennel bulb, quartered

20-cm strip of orange zest

2 litres boiling water

1 kg mixed fish fillets such as John Dory, red gurnard, red snapper, sea bass and grey mullet, cut into 4-cm chunks

1 kg mixed shellfish, such as small crabs, mussels, clams and prawns

a large pinch of saffron threads

500 g boiled new potatoes

1 tablespoon Pernod (optional)

4 tablespoons harissa paste or other hot chilli paste

1 baguette, sliced and oven-toasted to make croûtes

AIOLI

6–8 large garlic cloves, crushed

½ teaspoon sea salt

1 egg, plus 2 egg yolks

220 ml extra virgin olive oil

1–2 tablespoons freshly squeezed lemon juice

SERVES 4–6

This classic salad comes from the Isle of Capri in the Bay of Naples, where it is known as Insalata Caprese. It combines three ingredients that work beautifully in harmony with each other: mozzarella (preferably soft, creamy mozzarella di bufala), red, ripe tomato and plenty of fresh basil. To make this salad really sing of sunny Capri, use the best possible ingredients and be generous with them.

tomato, mozzarella and basil salad

Cut the mozzarella and tomatoes into slices about 5 mm thick. Arrange the tomato slices on a large plate and season with salt and pepper. Put 1 slice of mozzarella on each slice of tomato and top with a basil leaf. Tear up the remaining basil and scatter over the top. Drizzle with a generous amount of olive oil just before serving.

This salad must be made at the last moment to prevent the tomatoes from weeping and the mozzarella from drying out. Serve at room temperature, never chilled, as this would kill the flavours.

Variation Although not strictly Italian, sliced avocado is a delicious addition. Halve and peel one ripe avocado, remove the stone and slice the flesh, then intersperse the slices of avocado with the tomato and mozzarella.

2 balls of buffalo mozzarella, 150 g each

2 large, ripe tomatoes, roughly the same size as the balls of mozzarella

50 g fresh basil leaves

about 100 ml extra virgin olive oil

sea salt and freshly ground black pepper

SERVES 4

In Sicily, the land of orange and lemon groves, this salad is often served after grilled fish - especially in the region around Palermo. It is a perfect example of the Sicilian passion for sweet and savoury combinations and is very refreshing.

orange, escarole and black olive salad

To make the dressing, put the orange zest and juice, olive oil, basil, olives and sun-dried tomatoes in a large bowl. Mix well, season with salt and pepper and set aside to develop the flavours.

Peel the oranges with a sharp knife, removing all the skin and white pith. Cut out the segments. Set aside in a bowl. Finely slice the onion, using a very sharp thin-bladed knife. Immediately toss the onion and oranges in the dressing to prevent discoloration. Let marinate in a cool place for 15 minutes.

Put the escarole on a plate and pile the dressed orange and onion mixture in the centre, spooning over any remaining dressing. Serve immediately.

2 oranges

1 red onion

125 g escarole, curly endive or frisée

DRESSING

finely grated zest and freshly squeezed juice of 1 orange

6 tablespoons extra virgin olive oil

2 tablespoons thinly sliced fresh basil

2 tablespoons finely chopped, pitted, Greek-style, oven-dried black olives

2 sun-dried tomatoes in oil, finely chopped

sea salt and freshly ground black pepper

SERVES 4

salad of chicory leaves and blue cheese

200 g blue cheese, such as Spanish Cabrales or Picón, or French Roquefort

6 tablespoons whipping or single cream

6 heads of chicory or other crisp lettuce

3 tablespoons shelled walnuts, toasted in a dry frying pan and roughly broken

¼ teaspoon hot Spanish paprika

SERVES 4

This delicious Spanish salad is a mouthwatering combination of blue cheese, chicory and walnuts. A dusting of Spanish paprika adds an extra piquancy. Serve with chunks of crusty bread to mop up the creamy cheese dressing.

Put 150 g of the blue cheese in a bowl, then add the cream little by little, mixing to a smooth sauce.

Trim the bases from the chicory. Either cut them in half lengthways or separate the leaves. Add to the bowl of dressing. Sprinkle with the walnuts and crumble the remaining cheese over the top. Dust with paprika and serve.

Note Spanish paprika (*pimentón*) is available in three forms; *pimentón dulce* is mild and sweet, *pimentón picante* is spicy hot, while *pimentón agridulce* is bittersweet. There are also smoked versions which are made from chillies hung whole in traditional mud houses above oak fires that burn for 10–15 days. All these varieties are available in large supermarkets or specialist food shops.

Greek salads are so much part of the easy, Mediterranean style of eating – crisp lettuce, crumbly feta cheese, fragrant herbs, vinegary olives and salty anchovies thrown together in a bowl. Use unstoned Kalamata olives, if possible, as they have more flavour than other kinds, but warn your guests in case they're not expecting them.

1 iceberg lettuce, quartered and torn apart

about 250 g feta cheese, crumbled into big pieces or cut into cubes

about 200 g Kalamata olives

2 red onions, thinly sliced

2 mini cucumbers, halved lengthways, then thinly sliced diagonally

4 large tomatoes, cut into chunks

8 anchovy fillets, or to taste*

a few sprigs of oregano, torn

a few sprigs of mint, torn

DRESSING

6 tablespoons extra virgin olive oil

2 tablespoons freshly squeezed lemon juice

sea salt and freshly ground black pepper

SERVES 4

greek salad

Put the lettuce in a large bowl. Add the cheese, olives, onions, cucumbers and tomatoes.

To make the dressing, put the olive oil, lemon juice, salt and pepper in a jug or bowl and beat with a fork, then pour over the salad. Alternatively sprinkle the dressing ingredients onto the salad separately.

Top the salad with the anchovies, oregano and mint, and serve.

*Note Look out for big cans of salted anchovies in Greek markets and delicatessens – wheels of whole fish arranged nose to tail which you rinse and fillet yourself. If unavailable, use canned anchovy fillets.

warm mediterranean puy lentil salad

*This is a salad for all seasons, which uses the quintessential
Mediterranean flavourings of olive oil, lemon, garlic, and parsley.
It works wonderfully served warm or cold and is bound to become
a regular feature on your table.*

Put the cherry tomatoes on a lightly oiled baking sheet and cook in a preheated
oven at 130°C (250°F) for 40 minutes.

Put the lentils in a saucepan. Add the lemon rind and juice, bay leaf, garlic and
enough water to cover. Stir, bring to the boil, then simmer for 40 minutes or until
the lentils are soft.

Drain the lentils thoroughly and transfer to a large bowl. Add the tomatoes,
onion, olives, parsley, olive oil, salt and pepper. Toss gently, then serve topped
with slices of Parmesan.

Note This is not only a great salad but, with various additions, can also be
served as a whole meal in various ways. Try adding bacon or ham when cooking
the lentils, or some spicy sausage just before you mix everything together.

100 g cherry tomatoes

300 g Puy lentils or other
brown lentils

peeled rind and freshly
squeezed juice of 1 lemon

1 fresh bay leaf

2 garlic cloves, chopped

2 red onions, diced

75 g pitted green olives

a bunch of fresh flat leaf
parsley, coarsely chopped

4 tablespoons extra virgin
olive oil

sea salt and freshly ground
black pepper

100 g Parmesan or mozzarella
cheese, to serve

SERVES 4

grilled mixed vegetable salad with balsamic herb dressing

1 medium courgette

1 medium aubergine

1 large red pepper, halved and deseeded

12 tablespoons extra virgin olive oil

2 small red onions, quartered

150 g cherry tomatoes

2 teaspoons balsamic vinegar

1 garlic clove, crushed

3 tablespoons chopped mixed fresh herbs, such as parsley, basil, marjoram or oregano, plus extra to serve

sea salt and freshly ground black pepper

SERVES 4

This is one of the easiest ways to cook and serve a selection of Mediterranean vegetables for a large number of people. Grilling the vegetables concentrates their flavours, and a touch of aged balsamic vinegar cuts through their sweetness. Don't cut the vegetables too small – this salad should be robust and chunky.

Cut the courgette, aubergine and the pepper halves into large, bite-sized pieces. Transfer to a large bowl, add 6 tablespoons olive oil and toss well. Season to taste with salt and pepper.

Line a grill pan with aluminium foil and spoon in the vegetables. Add the onions and spread out the vegetables in an even layer (don't overcrowd the pan or they will stew). Grill under a preheated hot grill for 4–5 minutes or until the edges of the vegetables start to catch. Stir well, add the tomatoes and grill for a further 5 minutes until the vegetables are browned and cooked but not mushy.

Meanwhile, whisk the remaining olive oil with the balsamic vinegar, garlic and herbs. Pour the dressing over the vegetables, toss lightly and transfer to a serving dish. Cover and set aside for at least 30 minutes to let the flavours infuse. Serve sprinkled with extra herbs. Do not serve chilled as this will ruin the flavour.

85 g bulghur wheat

2 tomatoes, halved, cored and chopped, with the juices reserved

1 red onion or shallot, finely chopped and soaked in a little lemon juice

½ cucumber, peeled, deseeded and cut into cubes

2 tablespoons extra virgin olive oil

a pinch of cayenne pepper

1 teaspoon ground sumac or the freshly squeezed juice of ½ lemon*

a bunch of fresh flat leaf parsley

a bunch of fresh mint

sea salt and freshly ground black pepper

lemon and lime wedges, to serve

SERVES 2–4

This Turkish salad of bulghur wheat and herbs is similar to the more familiar Lebanese tabbouleh. Chop the mint last and add it to the salad just before serving, to prevent it turning black. Traditionally, this salad is served with pickled vegetables on boiled vine leaves, but it also works well served simply with lemon and lime wedges.

mint and parsley salad

Put the bulghur in a bowl and cover with 150 ml cold water. Let stand for about 40 minutes to absorb the liquid.

Put the bulghur in a sieve and squeeze out any excess water. Transfer to a serving bowl, then add the tomatoes and their juices, onion, cucumber, olive oil, cayenne, salt, pepper and half the sumac.

Remove the leaves from the parsley and mint and chop them coarsely. Add to the salad, toss gently and sprinkle with the remaining sumac. Serve with lemon and lime wedges.

*Note The reddish-purple sumac berry is a spice tasting a little of lemons. It is sold finely ground and is available from Middle Eastern stores and spice shops. If you can't find it, add the freshly squeezed juice of ½ lemon.

1–2 large garlic cloves, crushed

1 tablespoon sherry vinegar or white wine vinegar

6 tablespoons extra virgin olive oil

600 g cooked cannellini beans, rinsed and drained

2 red onions, thinly sliced, or 6 small spring onions, sliced

400 g good-quality tinned tuna

a few handfuls of fresh basil

sea salt and freshly ground black pepper

SERVES 6

This delicious antipasti of tuna and beans is a useful recipe when you're running low on fresh ingredients. Any dolphin-friendly canned tuna is fine, although top-quality French or Italian tuna, usually sold in jars, rather than cans, makes a special treat. Cannellini beans can be delicate, so toss them gently.

tonno e fagioli

Put the garlic on a chopping board, crush with the flat of a knife, add a large pinch of salt, then mash to a paste with the tip of the knife. Transfer to a bowl, add the vinegar and 2 tablespoons of the olive oil and beat with a fork.

Add the beans and onion and toss gently. Taste, then add extra olive oil and vinegar to taste.

Drain the tuna and separate into large chunks. Add to the bowl and turn gently to coat with the dressing. Top with the basil and some black pepper.

salade niçoise

The famous Salade Niçoise was originally composed of crudités with eggs and anchovies. Now served in cafés, restaurants and snack bars from New Zealand to Newfoundland, it is often made badly, with key ingredients left out or inappropriate ones added. Tuna, too costly for inclusion until recent times, can be fresh or canned, as long as it's of high quality. The anchovies can be salted, tinned or marinated, though marinated is really a Spanish innovation. Although this is a splendid main course dish, it is also appealing as a side salad if served in small quantities.

1 head cos lettuce, 3 Little Gems or one iceberg lettuce, leaves separated and halved if large

2 spring onions or shallots, sliced

250–350 g good-quality tinned tuna, drained

50 g tinned anchovies, or 24 marinated anchovy fillets, halved lengthways

12 black olives, such as Niçoise

4 hard-boiled large eggs, peeled and quartered

a handful of small sprigs of fresh flat leaf parsley or basil

4 ripe tomatoes, cut into 4–8 wedges

100 g green beans, halved, or shelled broad beans, freshly boiled

VINAIGRETTE

2 garlic cloves, crushed to a pulp

½ teaspoon sea salt

2 tablespoons wine vinegar

6–8 tablespoons extra virgin olive oil

SERVES 4

Line a large salad bowl with the lettuce leaves. Add the spring onions, tuna, anchovies, olives, egg quarters, parsley, tomatoes and beans.

To make the vinaigrette, put the garlic, salt, vinegar and olive oil in a bowl or bottle and beat or shake until emulsified. Pour over the salad just before serving.

The important thing with this chicken salad is to prepare it while the chicken is still warm. Pull the chicken breast into large pieces, rather than chopping it – it separates along the grain, tastes better and is more tender.

warm chicken salad with harissa dressing

Put the tomatoes onto a baking sheet – if using vine tomatoes, put the whole vine on the sheet. Sprinkle with salt, olive oil, and the crushed garlic, then roast in a preheated oven at 200°C (400°F) Gas 6, until slightly charred and starting to collapse. Let cool, but do not chill.

To make the harissa dressing, mix all of the ingredients in a salad bowl and beat with a fork.

While still warm, pull the chicken into long chunks. Add to the bowl, then add the leaves, olives and onion and toss gently in the dressing.

Divide between 4 salad plates, add the tomatoes and serve.

Notes As unstoned olives have more flavour than pitted ones, pit and halve them yourself. Choose any kind – with garlic, chilli, lemon and herbs – whatever looks good on the day. Brands of harissa paste vary in heat, so add a little, taste, then add more if you prefer. Alternatively, use regular mustard.

2 punnets ripe cherry tomatoes, or 4 sprays of cherry or plum tomatoes on the vine

½ garlic clove, crushed

4 freshly-cooked chicken breasts

salad leaves

20 large green or black olives, pitted and halved

2 red onions, halved, then cut into thin wedges lengthways

sea salt

olive oil, for roasting

HARISSA DRESSING

6 tablespoons extra virgin olive oil

1 tablespoon harissa paste

1 tablespoon cider or sherry vinegar

SERVES 4

This is one of the classics of French cooking and a perfect example of what is known as salade tiède or warm salad. It includes bitter leaves such as spinach, frisée and escarole, and the salad is topped with crisp bacon, in this case the French lardons. The cooking juices from the pine nuts, garlic and bacon are used to dress the salad.

french duck salade tiède

4 duck breasts

500 g baby spinach leaves

100 g pine nuts

3 garlic cloves, thinly sliced

250 g bacon lardons, pancetta cubes or thinly sliced smoked pancetta, as fatty as possible

olive oil, for frying

sea salt and freshly ground black pepper

VINAIGRETTE

6 tablespoons extra virgin olive oil

1 tablespoon red wine vinegar

sea salt and freshly ground black pepper

SERVES 4

Put the duck breasts skin side down in a frying pan lightly brushed with olive oil. Sprinkle the flesh side with a little sea salt. Cook gently over low heat for 20–30 minutes to render out the fat – you will have to pour it off from time to time into a heatproof bowl. Take it slowly – the skin will gradually become crisp and golden and the fat line will almost disappear.

Meanwhile, make the vinaigrette. Put all of the ingredients in a small bowl and beat with a fork.

Turn the duck over and cook at high heat just to brown the flesh side – the interior should remain rare. Remove from the pan and let rest for about 5 minutes if serving hot, or 20 minutes if serving cool. Carve crossways on a wooden board, making sure each slice has its share of crackling.

Put the spinach in a bowl, add the vinaigrette and toss lightly. Divide the leaves between 4 dinner plates or 8 starter plates.

Meanwhile, rinse and dry the frying pan. Reheat, add about 2 tablespoons olive oil, then the pine nuts. Toast over low heat, tossing gently, until golden on all sides, about 1 minute. Take care – they burn easily. Remove from the pan and let cool on a plate. Add the garlic to the pan and fry gently until crisp and golden brown. Remove to the same plate.

Add the bacon lardons and fry gently until crispy. Add the lardons to the salads, top with the pine nuts and garlic, then spoon the hot scented oil from the pan over the salads. Add freshly ground black pepper and serve.

fish and seafood

3 kg fresh mussels

4 tablespoons extra virgin olive oil

3 garlic cloves, very finely chopped

3 onions, very finely chopped

200 ml dry white wine

a good pinch of chilli flakes

4 tablespoons chopped fresh flat leaf parsley

TO SERVE

lemon wedges

warm French bread

a muslin-lined sieve

SERVES 6

In this classic French seafood dish, fresh mussels are cooked in white wine and flavoured with garlic and chilli. Take the pot to the table and ladle out the mussels first, then serve the delicious soupy juices to be mopped up with crusty bread. It is a is a dish to be shared with friends and savoured.

moules marinière

Scrub the mussels well, knock off any barnacles and pull off the beards. Discard any broken mussels and any that won't close when they are tapped on the work surface. Drain in a colander.

Heat the olive oil in a large saucepan. Add the garlic and onions and fry for 10 minutes until softened but not coloured. Add the wine, chilli flakes and 200 ml water, bring to the boil and simmer for another 10 minutes. Add the mussels, cover and cook over high heat for about 5 minutes, shaking the pan every now and then, until the mussels have opened. Discard any that remain closed. Strain the mussels through the muslin-lined sieve set over a bowl or saucepan.

Keep the mussels warm in the colander and boil the mussel liquid to reduce slightly. Stir in the parsley. Pile the mussels into warmed bowls, and pour over the hot broth. Serve with lemon wedges and bread to mop up the broth.

4 large garlic cloves, crushed

a bunch of fresh thyme or rosemary

12 clams or other bivalves

12 mussels

about 4 tablespoons extra virgin olive oil

2 large onions, cut into wedges through the root

8 ripe, very red tomatoes, skinned, halved and deseeded

1 kg thick boneless white fish fillets, such as cod

4–8 small whole fish, cleaned and scaled (optional)

8 uncooked prawns

1 litre boiling fish stock

sea salt and freshly ground black pepper

crusty Italian bread, to serve

a muslin-lined sieve

SERVES 4

A great dish with assertive flavours which is suitable for any occasion. You can alter the composition of this soup-stew according to what's available in your local market or supermarket, but be sure to include thick white fish, shellfish and prawns. Serve with fresh Italian bread and a jug of light red wine.

neapolitan seafood stew

Put 250 ml water into a large saucepan and add 1 crushed garlic clove and half the herbs. Bring to the boil, then simmer for 2–3 minutes to extract the flavours. Add the clams, cover with a lid and cook over high heat, shaking the pan from time to time. As they open, remove and put onto a plate, so they don't overcook. Discard any that don't open.

Add the mussels to the pan, cover with a lid and cook until they open. Remove as they do so and add to the plate with the clams. Discard any that don't open. Strain the cooking stock through the muslin-lined sieve into a bowl to remove the grit. Set aside.

Heat the olive oil in a large frying pan, add the onion wedges and cook until lightly browned on both sides. Reduce the heat and cook until softened. Stir in the remaining garlic and cook for a few minutes until golden. Add lots of black pepper, then add the tomatoes, the remaining herbs, both kinds of fish and the prawns. Pour in the stock and bring to boiling point. Reduce the heat and simmer for a few minutes until the fish turns opaque. Add the mussels, clams and the strained mussel poaching liquid. Reheat, then add salt and pepper.

Ladle into 4 large, warmed bowls and serve with crusty Italian bread.

Paella is the perfect dish for outdoor parties – everything can be prepared ahead of time, then you just add the ingredients in a steady stream until the whole thing comes together. The smell is wonderfully enticing, so make enough for seconds. This is messy food, so have plenty of paper napkins around.

paella

3 tablespoons extra virgin olive oil

6 chicken thighs

175 g chorizo sausage, cut into chunks

2 garlic cloves, finely chopped

1 large onion, finely chopped

1 large red pepper, thinly sliced

500 g Spanish paella rice

175 ml dry white wine

a good pinch of dried red chilli flakes

2 teaspoons sweet Spanish paprika (page 65)

about 1.2 litres chicken stock

a large pinch of saffron strands, soaked in 3 tablespoons hot water

6 ripe tomatoes, quartered

12 whole uncooked prawns, in their shells

500 g fresh mussels, scrubbed, rinsed and debearded

125 g fresh or frozen peas

4 tablespoons chopped fresh flat leaf parsley

sea salt and freshly ground black pepper

lime or lemon wedges, to serve

SERVES 6

Heat the olive oil in a paella pan or large, deep frying pan. Add the chicken thighs and chorizo and brown all over, turning frequently. Stir in the garlic, onion and red pepper and cook for about 5 minutes until softened.

Stir in the rice until all the grains are coated and glossy. Add the wine and let it bubble and reduce until almost disappeared. Stir in the chilli flakes, paprika, chicken stock and soaked saffron. Stir well, bring to the boil and simmer gently for 10 minutes.

Stir in the tomatoes and prawns and cook gently for 5 minutes before finally tucking the mussels into the rice and adding the peas. Cook for another 5 minutes until the mussels open (take out any that do not open after this time). At this stage, almost all the liquid will have been absorbed and the rice will be tender.

Sprinkle the parsley over the top and serve immediately, straight from the pan with a big pile of lime or lemon wedges on the side.

seafood with couscous

Couscous is probably Berber in origin and is found not only in North Africa, but also in Nice and other areas around the Mediterranean, such as Sicily, the home of this delicious recipe. The fish stew is ladled over aromatic cuscusu and the juices add their flavour to its fragrant charms. Modern 'instant' or pre-cooked couscous is quick and easy because it needs only moistening and heating, unlike cooking traditional North African couscous which requires skill and is very time-consuming.

1.5 kg assorted non-oily fish and shellfish, such as monkfish, red snapper, crayfish, lobster, prawns, crabs, mussels and clams

1 teaspoon sea salt

4 garlic cloves, sliced

4 celery stalks, sliced

1 head of fennel, quartered

20 black peppercorns, crushed

30-cm strip of orange zest

30-cm strip of lemon zest

a bunch of oregano or thyme

1–2 tablespoons tomato purée

CUSCUSU

500 g coarse instant couscous

1 onion, sliced

2 green chillies, thinly sliced

2 tablespoons extra virgin olive oil

750 ml boiling seafood stock or hot water

1 teaspoon orange flower water (optional)

freshly squeezed juice of 1 orange

sea salt and freshly ground black pepper

SERVES 4–6

Cut the fish and shellfish into 3-cm chunks or, if small, leave whole. Put them in a very large flameproof casserole, add the salt, garlic, celery, fennel, peppercorns and 500 ml water and bring to the boil. Stir in the orange and lemon zest, oregano, and enough tomato purée to make the liquid rosy. Reduce the heat to simmering. Cover and cook for 10 minutes.

To prepare the cuscusu, put the couscous, onion, chilli, olive oil, salt and pepper in a heatproof bowl. Pour in the boiling stock. Stir and leave for 5 minutes to plump up. Stir in the orange flower water, if using. When all the liquid has been absorbed, add the orange juice.

Put the cuscusu in deep bowls and serve the fish and its broth over the top.

600 g thick tuna steaks,
cut into 5-cm cubes

2-3 small red onions, quartered

2-3 mixed coloured peppers,
deseeded and sliced into
8 pieces each

5-6 sprigs of parsley, to serve

MARINADE

3 tablespoons olive oil

freshly squeezed juice of
1 large lemon

2 garlic cloves, crushed

1 green chilli, deseeded
and finely chopped

1 tablespoon dried oregano

1 teaspoon dried thyme

a handful of fresh parsley,
finely chopped

sea salt and freshly
ground black pepper

6 metal skewers

MAKES 6

Grilled fish is an integral part of Greek summer life and there is nothing more exhilarating than the aroma of barbecuing fish in the open air. Whenever the fishing boats bring in a large, glistening specimen, such as tuna or swordfish, it is inevitably made into kebabs by the local restaurants that evening. These tuna kebabs are a real treat at a barbecue and could be served with a selection of salads and dips, such as Greek Salad (page 66) and Babaghannouj (page 17).

grilled tuna kebabs

To make the marinade, put the olive oil, lemon juice, garlic, chilli, oregano, thyme, parsley, salt and pepper in a large bowl and beat well. Add the tuna pieces and stir to coat. Cover with clingfilm and chill in the refrigerator for 2-3 hours, stirring occasionally.

Separate the onion quarters into 2-3 pieces each, according to their size. Remove the tuna cubes from the marinade. Starting with a piece of pepper, thread pieces of tuna, onion and pepper onto a skewer, finishing with a piece of pepper. Repeat with the remaining skewers.

Barbecue over hot coals for 5-7 minutes on each side according to the strength of the fire, basting with the leftover marinade as they cook. Alternatively, cook under a preheated grill on all sides, about 10 cm from the heat, for 6-8 minutes in total. Take care as tuna can become dry if overcooked.

Meanwhile, put the remaining marinade into a small saucepan and boil for 2-3 minutes. To serve, arrange the skewers on a platter with sprigs of parsley and drizzle some of the leftover marinade juices over the top.

spanish fishcakes

Bacalao (salt cod) is the classic base for these fishcakes. You can also use smoked cod, smoked haddock or even smoked salmon instead, but if you use the traditional salt cod, it must be softened and desalted – put it in a bowl, cover with cold water and keep in the refrigerator for 24 hours, changing the water every 4 hours.

Cook the potatoes in boiling salted water for 20 minutes. Drain well, return to the still-hot empty saucepan and let dry.

Put the milk into a frying pan, bring to the boil, add the fish and poach gently until flaking and hot, about 6–8 minutes. Drain well, reserving the hot milk. Cool the fish, then skin, bone and flake it.

Add the flaked fish to the saucepan, then the olive oil, egg, spring onions, coriander, salt and pepper. Mix and mash to a dense texture, adding ½–1 tablespoon of the hot milk if necessary. Divide the mixture into 8–12 balls. Pat out into flat cakes, then coat in the seasoned flour.

Put 6 tablespoons olive oil in a non-stick frying pan and heat to 190°C (375°F) or until a 1-cm cube of bread browns in 35–45 seconds. Cook 3–4 fishcakes at a time for about 4 minutes on each side. Using a spatula and a slotted spoon, turn them carefully to avoid splashes. Drain on crumpled kitchen paper and keep hot while all the rest are cooked, adding some extra oil to the pan. Serve hot with lemon wedges.

500 g floury potatoes, halved lengthways

350 ml whole milk

350 g smoked haddock or cod, or desalted salt cod

2 tablespoons extra virgin olive oil

1 egg, beaten

4 spring onions, chopped

1 small bunch of fresh coriander, chopped, about 25 g

8 tablespoons plain flour seasoned with salt and pepper, to coat

olive oil, for frying

sea salt and freshly ground black pepper

lemon wedges, to serve

SERVES 4

12 fresh, fat sardines

olive oil, for brushing

lemon wedges, to serve

SALMORIGLIO SAUCE

2 tablespoons red wine vinegar

1–2 teaspoons sugar

finely grated zest and freshly
squeezed juice of ½ lemon

4 tablespoons extra virgin
olive oil

1 garlic clove, finely chopped

1 tablespoon crumbled
dried oregano

1 tablespoon salted capers,
rinsed and chopped

a barbecue grilling rack

SERVES 4

The smell of silvery blue sardines on a grill is unmistakable – it is one of the most appetizing scents in outdoor cooking. Sardines grill very well because they are an oily fish and are self-basting. There are wheel-shaped grilling racks especially designed for sardines. Great shoals of sardines are to be found in Mediterranean waters in May and June, when they are caught and eaten grilled, fried or stuffed.

grilled sardines with salmoriglio sauce

To make the salmoriglio sauce, put the vinegar and sugar in a bowl and stir to dissolve. Add the lemon zest and juice. Whisk in the olive oil, then add the garlic, oregano and capers. Set aside to infuse.

Using the back of a knife, scale the sardines, starting from the tail and working towards the head. Slit open the belly and remove the insides, then rinse the fish and pat dry. Clip off any fins you don't want to see. Brush the fish with olive oil and arrange on the grilling rack.

Cook under a preheated hot grill or barbecue over hot coals for about 3 minutes each side until sizzling hot and charring. Serve with the salmoriglio spooned over the top, with lots of lemon wedges alongside.

2 whole fish, about 750 g each, such as snapper, sea bass, sea bream or grey mullet, scaled, cleaned and fins trimmed

a few bay leaves

a few sprigs of fresh lemon thyme

2 tablespoons extra virgin olive oil, plus extra for basting

2 juicy lemons, halved

sea salt and freshly ground black pepper

CHERMOULA

1 teaspoon ground cumin

1 teaspoon ground coriander

a pinch of saffron threads

2 garlic cloves, chopped

1 teaspoon grated lemon zest

1 teaspoon mild Spanish paprika, preferably oak-smoked (page 65)

2 tablespoons chopped fresh flat leaf parsley

3 tablespoons chopped fresh coriander

freshly squeezed juice of 1 lemon

4 tablespoons extra virgin olive oil

cayenne or chilli powder, to taste

sea salt and freshly ground black pepper

SERVES 4

Chermoula is a Moroccan spice paste or marinade fragrant with coriander, garlic, lemon and spices. It is a useful flavouring to know, as it is wonderfully adaptable, working equally well with fish, lamb or chicken. Grilling the lemon releases the juice and mellows its flavour, making it perfect for squeezing over the grilled fish.

grilled fish with chermoula and grilled lemons

To make the chermoula, put the cumin, ground coriander and saffron in a small saucepan and heat gently for 1 minute to release the aromas. Transfer to a small food processor or spice mill, then add the garlic, lemon zest, paprika, parsley and fresh coriander and finely chop. Add the lemon juice and olive oil and blend to make a paste. Add a little cayenne, and salt and pepper to taste, cover and set aside for 30 minutes.

Season the cavities of the fish with salt. Cut 4 or 5 diagonal, shallow slashes on each side of the fish and work a little chermoula into each cut. Lay the fish in a heatproof dish and stuff a few bay leaves and a little thyme into the cavities. Cover and let stand in the refrigerator for 30–60 minutes.

Season the fish with salt and pepper and sprinkle with the olive oil, then put under a preheated overhead grill, with the rack set about 10 cm from the heat. Grill for about 5 minutes on each side or until the fish is just cooked at the centre – test with the tip of a pointed knife. When you turn the fish, add the lemon halves, cut side up, and baste them with a little extra oil. Grill until the cut surface of the lemons is nicely brown and the fish cooked. Serve the fish and lemons immediately with any remaining chermoula.

Note You can barbecue both fish and lemons. Use a special wire fish grilling rack, which makes turning the fish easier. Oil the rack slightly and allow up to 10 minutes each side, depending on the heat of the coals and the size of the fish. Place the lemon halves directly on the barbecue or, alternatively, cook them on a ridged stove-top grill pan for 2–3 minutes until the cut surfaces are seared.

4 tuna steaks, 175 g each

40 g Cheddar cheese, cut into
4 thin slices

sea salt and freshly ground
black pepper

salad leaves or buttered
spinach, to serve

PAPRIKA CRUMBS

1 tablespoon olive oil

50 g fresh white breadcrumbs

1 tablespoon chopped fresh basil

½ teaspoon hot oak-smoked
Spanish paprika (page 65)

1 teaspoon tomato purée

½ teaspoon sugar

ROMESCO SAUCE

2 red peppers

100 ml olive oil

2 garlic cloves

1 red chilli, deseeded and sliced

200 g tinned plum tomatoes

25 ml red wine vinegar

1 tablespoon ground hazelnuts

1 tablespoon ground almonds

1 teaspoon sea salt

SERVES 4

*Tuna is a dark-fleshed fish that needs extra flavouring and takes well
to hot paprika seasoning. The topping gives a moist and crunchy
texture to a fish that can become dry and overcooked only too easily.
Serve on a bed of salad leaves or buttered spinach with romesco
sauce – a hot, pungent, Catalan sauce thickened with ground almonds
and hazelnuts, which is often served with fish and can also be used
as a dip for crudités.*

tuna with paprika crumbs and romesco sauce

To make the romesco sauce, char-grill the peppers under a preheated hot grill,
then put them in a paper bag, seal and let steam for 10 minutes. Remove the
skin, seeds and membranes. Heat 1 teaspoon of the olive oil in a non-stick pan,
lightly brown the garlic, then add the chilli and tomatoes. Dry out the mixture
over high heat so it starts to fry and even brown a little. Transfer to a blender,
add the vinegar and remaining oil, and purée until smooth. Stir in the nuts to
thicken the sauce and add salt to taste.

To make the paprika topping, put the olive oil in a frying pan, add the
breadcrumbs, basil, paprika, tomato purée, sugar and ½ teaspoon salt. Stir well
and fry until crunchy. Remove from the pan and let cool.

Season the tuna with salt and pepper, put on an oiled baking tray and roast
in a preheated oven at 250°C (475°F) Gas 9 for 5 minutes.

Remove from the oven and turn over the steaks. Pile the paprika breadcrumbs
on top, then add the slice of cheese. Return to the oven and cook for a further
5 minutes or until the cheese has melted. Serve on a bed of salad leaves or
buttered spinach, with the sauce served separately.

braised sea bass with fennel and green olives

This is the perfect way to cook a whole firm-fleshed fish. It keeps the flesh moist, while the skin protects it. Fennel and olives are distinctive Mediterranean flavours and a winning combination.

Wash the fish inside and out and fill the cavity with sprigs of rosemary.

Cut the fennel bulbs in half lengthways, cut out the cores, then slice thickly. Blanch in a large saucepan of salted boiling water for 5 minutes, then drain.

Put the olive oil, lemon juice and herbs in a medium bowl and season with salt and pepper. Whisk well, then stir in the fennel to coat. Tip this mixture into a shallow ovenproof dish. Put the fish on top of the fennel and pour over any remaining liquid. Tuck in the olives and pour the wine over the top.

Bake in a preheated oven at 220°C (425°F) Gas 7 for 30 minutes. Baste with the juices and stir the fennel around, then turn off the oven and leave for about 5 minutes for the fish to 'set'. Serve immediately.

1.25 kg sea bass or sea bream, scaled and cleaned

a few sprigs of rosemary

2 large fennel bulbs

150 ml extra virgin olive oil

freshly squeezed juice of 1 lemon

1 tablespoon dried oregano

3 tablespoons chopped fresh flat leaf parsley

8 large green olives, pitted

150 ml dry white wine

sea salt and freshly ground black pepper

SERVES 4

1 kg monkfish tail

sea salt and freshly ground black pepper

olive oil, for brushing

NIÇOISE SAUCE

200 g tinned tomatoes or 6 fresh tomatoes, skinned and deseeded

2 garlic cloves, crushed

2 tablespoons olive oil

125 ml white wine

250 ml fish stock

leaves from 2–3 sprigs of thyme, chopped

leaves from 2–3 small sprigs of tarragon, chopped

2 fresh sage leaves

1 bay leaf

sea salt and freshly ground black pepper

TO SERVE

12 black olives, chopped

fennel fronds

an instant-read thermometer

SERVES 4

This is usually made with a whole, large monkfish tail but cutlets or even four individual tails may be used instead. Adding cream to the Niçoise sauce makes an unusual variation, while black olives and fennel fronds add colour to the dish. Serve with rice.

roast gigot of monkfish with niçoise sauce

To make the Niçoise sauce, put the tomatoes, garlic and olive oil in a saucepan, bring to the boil, reduce the heat and simmer until they cook to a pulp – crush them from time to time. Add the wine and keep simmering until it has been absorbed by the tomatoes. Add the stock, thyme, tarragon, sage, bay leaf, salt and pepper.

Peel the skin off the monkfish and cut away the loose membrane. Shorten the tail with scissors but do not cut into the flesh or it will shrink back and expose the bone as it cooks. Brush the fish with the oil and season with salt and pepper.

Spoon half the sauce into a roasting tin, rest the fish on it and roast in a preheated oven at 180°C (350°F) Gas 4 for 10 minutes. Turn the fish over and continue to cook until an instant-read thermometer registers 58°C (136°F), about 10 minutes. Transfer the fish to a serving dish and keep it warm.

Pour the roasting juices back into the saucepan of Niçoise sauce, bring to the boil and simmer until reduced to a pulp. Add salt and pepper to taste.

Pour the sauce around the fish, add the olives and fennel fronds and serve.

The rose and gold skin of the red mullet looks beautiful with the deep red of the blood oranges. If you can't find this fish, try red snapper and regular oranges instead. Citrus fruits are often cooked with fish in Italy – their gentle acidity brings out the sweetness of the flesh. You could also add a tablespoon of wine to each serving if tempted. The aroma when you open the packets is wonderful.

red mullet and orange parcels

4 red mullet or small red snapper, 250 g each, carefully scaled, cleaned and filleted

2 tablespoons extra virgin olive oil, plus extra for brushing

2 oranges, preferably blood oranges

8 fresh bay leaves

20 small black olives

sea salt and freshly ground black pepper

SERVES 4

Cut 4 rectangles of aluminium foil or baking parchment large enough to wrap each fish loosely. Brush with a little oil.

Grate the zest from the oranges into a bowl, then mix in the olive oil, salt and pepper and set aside. Peel the oranges as you would an apple, removing all the white pith, then slice the flesh thinly. Put 1 bay leaf in the cavity of each fish and 1 on top. Put a pile of orange slices on one side of each square of foil, using half the orange slices in total. Put the fish on the oranges and cover them with the remaining orange slices. Sprinkle with the oil and orange zest mixture, then add the olives. Season well with salt and pepper.

If you have a water sprayer, spritz the inside of the foil lightly. Fold the foil loosely over the fish and twist the edges together. Lift onto a baking tray. Bake in a preheated oven at 190°C (375°F) Gas 5 for 20 minutes.

Serve on warm plates, letting guests open their own packets.

hake in garlic sauce with clams

This fish dish is traditionally cooked in cazuela – a wide, flat, terracotta casserole, glazed except for the base. It has amazing heat-retaining properties and is excellent for dishes that rely on slow, even heat. If cooking on top of the stove, use a heat-diffusing mat.

Put the clams and wine in a saucepan over high heat. As they open, remove them to a bowl and cover with clingfilm. Discard any that don't open. Pour the cooking juices through the muslin-lined sieve and set aside. Put the fish on a plate, sprinkle with salt and leave to rest for 10 minutes.

Put the oil and garlic in a heavy frying pan and heat gently so the garlic turns golden slowly and doesn't burn. Remove the garlic with a slotted spoon and keep until ready to serve.

Pour about two-thirds of the oil into a jug and add the fish to the oil left in the pan. Cook over very low heat, moving the pan in a circular motion – keep taking it off the heat so it doesn't cook too quickly (the idea is to encourage the oozing of the juices instead of letting them fry and burn). Add the remaining oil little by little as you move the pan, so an emulsion starts to form. When all the oil has been added, remove the fish to a plate and keep it warm. Put the pan back on the heat, add the reserved clam juices and stir to form a creamy sauce.

Return the fish to the pan, add the chopped parsley and continue to cook until the fish is tender, about 5 minutes. Just before serving, add the clams and heat through. Serve sprinkled with black pepper and the fried garlic.

500 g clams

90 ml dry white wine

6 hake or cod steaks, cut 2 cm thick through the bone

150 ml olive oil

4 garlic cloves, thinly sliced

4 tablespoons chopped fresh flat leaf parsley

sea salt and freshly ground black pepper

a muslin-lined sieve

a heavy frying pan

SERVES 4–6

125 ml extra virgin olive oil

2 onions, halved and thinly sliced

2 garlic cloves, chopped

1–2 pinches of dried red chilli flakes

1 teaspoon crushed coriander seeds

½ teaspoon dried oregano

750 g waxy potatoes, peeled and cut into wedges

2 bay leaves

5 tablespoons white wine or vermouth

½ teaspoon grated lemon zest

700–750 g white fish (on or off the bone), cut into large chunks or steaks

2 small lemons, halved

1 tablespoon chopped fresh oregano

1 tablespoon chopped fresh flat leaf parsley

sea salt and freshly ground black pepper

a large frying pan or ovenproof skillet with a lid

a large ovenproof baking dish (optional)

SERVES 4

If you have a stovetop-to-oven pan, this dish can be cooked all in one pot. Use chunks of white fish such as monkfish, hake, snapper, grouper, bass or huss and choose potatoes that don't break up on cooking – large, waxy salad potatoes are ideal. As a rule of thumb, yellow-fleshed potatoes are waxy, while white potatoes tend to be floury. Some steamed greens tossed in a little olive oil make a great accompaniment to this dish.

fish baked with lemon, oregano and potatoes

Heat a large frying pan or ovenproof skillet over medium heat and add the oil. Add the onion and fry for 2–3 minutes, then turn the heat down low. Add 1–2 pinches of salt, cover and let the onion cook very gently for 10–12 minutes until soft and golden yellow. Add the garlic, chilli flakes, crushed coriander seeds and dried oregano. Cook for another 3–4 minutes.

Add the potatoes and bay leaves to the pan, turning them in the oily onions. Season with 1 teaspoon salt and several turns of the pepper mill, cook for a few minutes, then add the wine and lemon zest. When it bubbles, cover and cook gently for 15–20 minutes or until the potatoes are just tender.

Transfer the potatoes to a large ovenproof baking dish, if necessary. Season the fish with a little salt, then nestle the fish into the potatoes. Squeeze a little lemon juice from one of the lemon halves over the fish and spoon over a little of the oily juices. Add the lemon halves to the dish and turn in the oil.

Bake, uncovered, in a preheated oven at 200°C (400°F) Gas 6 for 20–25 minutes, basting once or twice, until the potatoes are fully tender and the fish cooked through. The lemons should be touched with brown. Serve immediately, sprinkled with the fresh oregano and parsley.

meat and poultry

provençal roasted chicken
with garlic, lemons and olives

Corn-fed chicken, salty olives and an intense lemon and garlic sauce make this French-style dish distinctive. Choose an olive oil which relates well to the olives and garlic: a lusty, green, fruity, Provençal oil would be perfect. You can also leave the lemon and garlic heads whole and serve a portion to each guest with a spoonful of the juice, rather than making the puréed sauce.

1.25–1.5 kg free-range, corn-fed chicken

3 tablespoons extra virgin olive oil

2 lemons

1 large bunch of fresh thyme

175 g black olives, such as dry-cured Provençal

4 whole heads of garlic

125 ml full-bodied red wine (optional)

sea salt and freshly ground black pepper

SERVES 4

Pat the chicken dry with kitchen paper. Rub the skin with a little olive oil and sprinkle with salt inside and out. Put, breast side down, in a roasting tin.

Slice the lemons crossways in a series of parallel slashes, but leave them attached at the base. Put half the thyme and one of the lemons inside the cavity and push more thyme between the trussed legs and underneath the bird. Push the olives under the bird. Add the remaining lemon to the tin.

Slice a 'lid' off the top of each garlic head. Drizzle 1 teaspoon olive oil over each one and replace the lids. Brush the remaining oil over the chicken and lemon.

Roast the chicken, breast side down, in a preheated oven at 220°C (425°F) Gas 7 for 40 minutes. Turn the bird on its back, put the prepared garlic heads underneath and roast for a further 35–40 minutes until deep golden brown. Prick the thigh at the thickest part – the juices should run a clear yellow. If there is any trace of pink, roast a little longer. Remove the chicken and olives from the pan. Let stand, covered, in a warm place for 8–10 minutes while you make the sauce (optional).

Pour off the pan juices from the tin. Measure 25 ml of the stickiest, darkest juices and put in a food processor. Add the wine, if using. Press the soft, creamy centres out of the garlic heads and add to the food processor. Tip up the bird and let the juices run into the food processor. Add a quarter of the roasted lemon, pulled into pieces. Whizz, in bursts, to a rich sauce. Taste and add extra stock if necessary. Gently simmer until the raw taste of wine has mellowed, about 3–5 minutes. Serve with the chicken.

chicken tagine with apricots

Many Moroccan dishes are seasoned with subtle spice combinations, mixed to order in the souk or bazaar. This chicken dish uses only four spices, two of which are used to rub into the skin of the chicken. If you can't find real saffron powder, double the amount of paprika and use half of that to help colour the chicken. The apricots grow plump and juicy with blanching and give the chicken dish a good balance of sweet, salty and sour flavours.

Mix the turmeric with the saffron, then rub it all over the chicken pieces. Put the apricots in a small saucepan, add 250 ml boiling water, bring very gently to the boil, cover with a lid, then simmer for about 10 minutes.

Heat the butter in a large flameproof casserole, then add the onions and sauté for 5 minutes, stirring. Add the ginger, paprika, peppercorns and salt. Put the chicken on top.

Add 350 ml cold water to the apricots, then pour the apricots and their liquid over and around the chicken.

Add the parsley, bring to the boil, cover with a lid, then reduce to a simmer and cook, undisturbed, for 20 minutes. Add the apple. Simmer for a further 10–15 minutes, adding a little extra water if it looks too dry (the fruit absorbs much of the water).

Remove and discard the parsley. Serve the tagine with couscous or plain rice, topped with a few mint sprigs, if using.

½ teaspoon ground turmeric

½–1 teaspoon saffron powder

1.5 kg chicken, cut into 8 or 10 pieces

250 g dried apricots

3 tablespoons butter or olive oil

2 onions, chopped

½ teaspoon ground ginger

½ teaspoon paprika

½ teaspoon crushed black peppercorns

1 teaspoon sea salt

a handful of fresh parsley, tied with string

1 cooking apple, such as Granny Smith, cored but not peeled, then cut into 8 pieces

TO SERVE

fresh mint sprigs

couscous or plain rice

SERVES 4

1.5 kg chicken, whole or
quartered, or 4 breast
or leg portions

2 tablespoons extra virgin
olive oil

10 whole cloves

20 pearl onions or
10 shallots, halved

8 canned artichokes, drained

4 garlic cloves, chopped

2 tablespoons white wine
vinegar or freshly squeezed
lemon juice

6 tablespoons rich tomato purée
(double strength)

450 g tinned chopped tomatoes

24 black olives, such as Kalamata

a large bunch fresh or dried
rosemary, oregano, thyme,
or a mixture

2 tablespoons Greek Metaxa
brandy (optional)

freshly ground black pepper

SERVES 4

In Greece stifado (or stifatho) can refer to a number of things, but essentially it is a thickened stew with tomato, garlic and olive oil – perfect for winter. Sometimes made with beef or rabbit, guinea fowl or even quail, it is easy to prepare and fragrant with herbs. The flambé is an unusual touch – entirely optional, but fun, especially if you use Metaxa brandy. Serve from the dish, accompanied with torn country bread, noodles, rice or even chips.

greek chicken stifado

Pat the chicken dry with kitchen paper. Heat the olive oil in a large flameproof casserole, add the chicken and sauté for 8–10 minutes, turning it with tongs from time to time.

Push the cloves into some of the onions and add them all to the pan. Add the artichokes, garlic, vinegar, tomato purée, tomatoes, olives and freshly ground black pepper. Tuck in the herb sprigs around the edges.

Bring to the boil and reduce the heat to low. Cover and simmer for 30 minutes for chicken pieces, or about 60 minutes if using a whole bird, or until the chicken seems tender and the sauce has reduced and thickened.

Heat the brandy in a warmed ladle, if using, and pour it, flaming, over the stifado.

Note If you have access to a wine merchant who sells Greek wine, try the unusual mavrodaphne – sweet, red and almost port-like.

Liver, along with other kinds of offal, has always been a delicacy in Mediterranean kitchens, especially in Greece, Italy and Spain, where it can be served as a kebab, a starter or a main dish. It is often cooked simply, with few spices or herbs. Lamb's liver, in small pieces, or halved chicken livers, are both appropriate for this recipe. Herb-flavoured rice and seasonal greens, cooked then dressed with olive oil and a squeeze of lemon are typical accompaniments.

chicken liver and bacon wraps

350 g chicken livers
or lamb's liver

1 nutmeg

8 slices thin, rindless streaky
bacon, preferably smoked,
halved lengthways

2 tablespoons extra virgin
olive oil

6 tablespoons red wine or
sweet red vermouth

4 tablespoons passata tomatoes

4 tablespoons chicken or lamb
stock, or water

sea salt and freshly ground
black pepper

cocktail sticks

SERVES 4

Use scissors to cut whole chicken livers into 2–4 pieces, discarding the membranous parts or any discoloured areas. If using lamb's liver, cut it into 1-cm thick slices and then into 2-cm pieces, about 25 g each. Pat the liver pieces dry with kitchen paper and dust with salt and pepper. Coarsely grate half the nutmeg and sprinkle over the liver, then wrap the bacon strips around each pair of liver pieces, using cocktail sticks to secure them.

Heat the olive oil in a large, non-stick frying pan and sauté the liver and bacon wraps for 1½–2 minutes on each side or until the bacon fat is translucent, the liver golden and the texture firm, but not hard. Push the meat to one side of the pan.

Put the remaining nutmeg piece in the pan with the wine, passata and stock. Cook, stirring over medium heat to dissolve the sediment on the base of the pan, to make a sauce. Turn the liver briefly in the sauce and reheat gently for 1 minute, then serve.

This classic recipe originates from Andalucia, in southern Spain, where both ducks and olive groves are plentiful. Any variety of black or green olive will work here and they will taste even better if you pit them yourself.

duck with olives

Put the duck in a shallow dish, sprinkle with the thyme, sherry, salt and pepper, and let marinate for about 30 minutes.

Pat the duck dry with kitchen paper and heat a frying pan on high heat until smoking. Add the duck skin side down and fry without oil, on one side only, for 5 minutes until deep golden brown. Remove the duck to a plate. Drain off the duck fat and keep to cook potatoes on another occasion. Wipe the pan, heat 1 tablespoon of the olive oil, add the shallots and fry until pale golden. Transfer to the plate with the duck.

Heat the remaining oil, add the onions and garlic and fry gently for 5 minutes until softened but not coloured. Increase the heat, add the wine and bring to the boil. Transfer to a shallow ovenproof casserole dish, add the shallots and duck breasts, skin side up, and the marinade. Cook in a preheated oven at 220°C (425°F) Gas 7 for 5–8 minutes. If you prefer the duck to be more well done, cook for 3–5 minutes longer.

Add the olives and cook for a further 5 minutes. Slice the duck breasts lengthways, then serve with the olive and onion mixture.

4 duck breasts, the fat scored into diamonds

4 sprigs of fresh thyme

2 tablespoons manzanilla sherry

3 tablespoons olive oil

10 shallots, separated into lobes

2 medium onions, finely chopped

3 garlic cloves, crushed

4 tablespoons dry white wine

20 black and 20 green olives, flesh sliced off the pits in 4 long pieces

sea salt and freshly ground black pepper

SERVES 4

This hearty dish from south-west France is ideal for large gatherings on cold winter days. It is traditionally made with a type of haricot bean called lingot, but the creamy texture of butter beans also works well. All the components of the dish can be made days in advance, then assembled on the day. It reheats very well – simply top up with a little more liquid if it looks dry.

675 g dried butter beans, or other white beans

500 g smoked Italian pancetta, fat bacon or belly pork, in a piece

4 tablespoons olive oil

4 boneless duck breasts, halved crossways, or chicken legs or thighs

750 g fresh Toulouse sausages or Italian coarse pork sausages, cut into 3 pieces each

2 medium onions, chopped

1 large carrot, chopped

4–6 large garlic cloves, crushed

3 bay leaves

2 teaspoons dried thyme

2 whole cloves

3 tablespoons tomato purée

12 sun-dried tomatoes in oil, drained and coarsely chopped

75 g fresh white breadcrumbs

50 g butter

sea salt and freshly ground black pepper

SERVES 6–8

cassoulet

The night before, put the beans in a very large bowl, cover with plenty of cold water (to cover them by their depth again) and let soak for several hours or according to the packet instructions.

The next day, drain the beans well and tip into a large saucepan. Cover with fresh water, bring to the boil, then simmer for about 1 hour or until just cooked. Drain well (reserving the cooking liquid).

Trim and discard the rind from the pancetta, and cut the flesh into large pieces. Heat 2 tablespoons of the olive oil in a frying pan, brown the pieces in batches and transfer to a plate. Heat the remaining oil in the pan, add the duck breasts and fry skin side down until the skin is golden. Transfer to the same plate as the pancetta. Brown the sausages in the same way and add to the plate. Add the onions to the pan, then the carrot, garlic, bay leaves, dried thyme, cloves, tomato purée and sun-dried tomatoes. Cook for 5 minutes until softening.

Put half the beans in a large, deep casserole. Add an even layer of all the meats, then the onion and tomato mixture. Season well with salt and pepper. Cover with the remaining beans, then add enough reserved hot cooking liquid so that the beans are almost covered. Sprinkle evenly with breadcrumbs and dot with butter. Bake the cassoulet in a preheated oven at 180°C (350°F) Gas 4 for about 1 hour until a golden crust has formed, then serve.

Souvlaki is the classic Greek kebab, a delicious combination of cubed lamb marinated in red wine with herbs and lemon juice. The meat is tenderized by the wine, resulting in a juicy and succulent dish.

souvlaki with bulghur wheat salad

Trim any large pieces of fat from the lamb and then cut the meat into 2.5-cm cubes. Put into a shallow, non-metal dish. Add the rosemary, oregano, onion, garlic, wine, lemon juice, olive oil, salt and pepper. Toss well, cover and let marinate in the refrigerator for 4 hours. Return to room temperature for 1 hour before cooking.

To make the salad, soak the bulghur wheat in warm water for 30 minutes until the water has been absorbed and the grains have softened. Strain well to extract any excess water and transfer the wheat to a bowl. Add all the remaining ingredients, season with salt and pepper, to taste, and let rest for 30 minutes to develop the flavours.

Thread the lamb onto large rosemary stalks or metal skewers. Barbecue over hot coals for 10 minutes, or cook under a preheated grill, turning and basting from time to time. Let rest for 5 minutes, then serve with the salad.

1 kg neck end of lamb

1 tablespoon chopped fresh rosemary

1 tablespoon dried oregano

1 onion, chopped

4 garlic cloves, chopped

300 ml red wine

freshly squeezed juice of 1 lemon

75 ml olive oil

sea salt and black pepper

BULGHUR WHEAT SALAD

350 g bulghur wheat

25 g fresh parsley, chopped

15 g fresh mint leaves

2 garlic cloves, crushed

150 ml extra virgin olive oil

freshly squeezed juice of 2 lemons

a pinch of caster sugar

sea salt and black pepper

6 large rosemary stalks or metal skewers

SERVES 6

Salsa Salmoretta is a spicy sauce from the Valencia and Alicante region of Spain and makes the perfect accompaniment to grilled or barbecued lamb cutlets. Pork chops are equally delicious marinaded and cooked in this way.

lamb cutlets with salsa salmoretta

To marinate the cutlets, put the garlic, paprika, thyme sprigs and leaves, olive oil, salt and pepper in a flat dish and stir to mix. Add the cutlets, turn to coat, and let marinate for 2 hours or overnight.

Heat a ridged stove-top grill pan until smoking, then add the cutlets and cook for 3 minutes on each side. Alternatively, barbecue over hot coals.

Meanwhile, to make the salsa salmoretta, put the shallot in a bowl and cover with cold water.

Cut a cross in the top of each tomato and put under a preheated hot grill for 5 minutes, turning twice, until the skins are wrinkled and the flesh is soft. Peel, deseed and finely chop the flesh, then put in a bowl.

Meanwhile, crush the garlic, chilli and parsley to a paste with a mortar and pestle. Work in two-thirds of the chopped tomatoes. Drain the shallot and crush half of it with the tomatoes. Still stirring with the pestle, gradually add the oil to emulsify. Stir in the vinegar, the remaining tomatoes and shallot, salt and pepper.

Serve the salsa with the cutlets.

3 garlic cloves, crushed

2 teaspoons sweet Spanish paprika (page 65)

4 sprigs of fresh thyme (leaves picked off 2 of them)

3 tablespoons olive oil

12 lamb cutlets, trimmed

sea salt and freshly ground black pepper

SALSA SALMORETTA

1 large shallot, thinly sliced

3 ripe medium tomatoes

2 garlic cloves, finely chopped

1 dried hot red chilli, deseeded and finely chopped

1 tablespoon finely chopped fresh flat leaf parsley

90 ml olive oil

1½ teaspoons red wine vinegar

sea salt and freshly ground black pepper

a ridged stove-top grill pan (optional)

SERVES 4

STUFFING

3 tablespoons olive oil

2 large onions, finely chopped

600 g minced lamb

1 teaspoon ground allspice

1 teaspoon ground cinnamon

2 tablespoons pomegranate syrup or 2 tablespoons freshly squeezed lemon juice

150 ml hot water

3–4 tablespoons pine nuts, toasted in a dry frying pan

4 tablespoons chopped fresh parsley

sea salt and freshly ground black pepper

KIBBEH

225 g fine bulghur wheat

1 large onion

500 g finely minced beef or lamb

1 teaspoon ground allspice

1 teaspoon ground cinnamon

100 g butter

sea salt and freshly ground black pepper

a selection of salads, to serve

a roasting tin, 30 x 24 x 5 cm, generously buttered

MAKES 12 PIECES

Kibbeh has an almost mythical status in Lebanese cooking. Before food processors appeared, it involved a lot of manual pounding, so it was mostly made for special occasions – not so now. Lebanese cooks decorate the top with intricate patterns before baking, but you can simply score it with a sharp knife to mark the portions.

baked kibbeh

To make the stuffing, heat the olive oil in a saucepan, add the onions and sauté until they start to turn golden. Increase the heat, add the meat and sauté until the moisture has evaporated and it starts to sizzle, 10–12 minutes. Add the allspice and cinnamon and fry for 2–3 minutes. Add salt, pepper, the pomegranate syrup and hot water, then cover and simmer for 30 minutes. Remove from the heat and stir in the pine nuts and parsley.

To make the kibbeh, soak the bulghur wheat in a bowl of cold water for 10 minutes. Change the water once and soak for another 5 minutes. Drain.

Put the onion in a food processor and pulse until finely chopped. Add the minced lamb, allspice, cinnamon, salt and pepper. Process until smooth. Transfer to a bowl and add the drained bulghur wheat. Have a bowl of cold water with some ice cubes in it ready. Wet your hand in the cold water and knead the mixture for a few minutes. Divide the kibbeh mixture into 2 portions.

Dip your hands in the cold water, take a small handful from one of the kibbeh portions, flatten it between your palms and spread it neatly at the base of the roasting tin. Continue, wetting your hands and joining the pieces neatly and overlapping slightly until the whole base is covered to about 1 cm thick.

Spread the stuffing evenly over the base. Use the other portion of kibbeh mixture to cover the top in the same way as before. Score the top with a sharp knife into diamond, rectangular or square serving portions. Dot the butter over the top and bake in a preheated oven at 180°C (350°F) Gas 4 for 20–30 minutes. (Do not overcook or it will become very dry.) Run a sharp knife around the edges, then cut the pieces carefully and lift individually onto a platter. Serve hot or at room temperature with a selection of salads.

moroccan butterflied and barbecued lamb

Moroccan lamb is one of the best and easiest meat dishes for a big barbecue party. Butterflied lamb is just a leg of lamb that has been split open and the bones removed so that it is flat and an even thickness. A butcher can do this for you. After marinating, the leg can be cooked like one huge steak in much less time than cooking a whole leg, and is easy to carve for large numbers.

Trim any excess fat from the lamb and score the meat where necessary to make it all the same thickness. Make deep slits all over the meat.

Put the peppercorns, coriander and cumin seeds and paprika in a dry frying pan, toast for a couple of minutes until aromatic, then grind or crush them. Transfer to a bowl, add the thyme, lime juice, garlic, yoghurt and salt to taste, then rub all over the cut side of the meat. Put in a shallow dish, cover and let marinate in the refrigerator for at least 1 hour.

Barbecue the lamb skin side down over medium-hot coals for 10–12 minutes, then turn and cook for a further 10–12 minutes for medium rare. (For medium, cook for a total of 30–35 minutes, and for well done, cook for a total of 40 minutes.)

Alternatively, cook the lamb on a foil-lined rack under a preheated medium-hot grill for 20 minutes, then turn and continue for a further 20 minutes (the meat should be medium).

When cooked, remove from the heat, cover loosely with foil and set aside in a warm place to rest for 10 minutes. Carve into long, thin slices. Serve with grilled flatbreads, salad and minted yoghurt.

2 kg leg of lamb, butterflied

1 tablespoon black peppercorns

1 tablespoon coriander seeds

1 tablespoon cumin seeds

1 tablespoon sweet Spanish paprika (page 65)

2 teaspoon dried thyme

freshly squeezed juice of 1 lime

2 garlic cloves, crushed

100 ml plain yoghurt

sea salt

TO SERVE

grilled flatbreads

salad

plain yoghurt mixed with chopped fresh mint

SERVES 6–8

luganega country sausage with lentils and wilted greens

Loukanika (Greece) and luganega (Italy) are similar types of sausage and have been known since antiquity. They contain fresh, coarse-cut pork and/or minced beef with salt, sugar, orange, chilli, cumin or aniseed, and coriander, with plenty of garlic, red wine and olive oil. This is all packed inside a long, traditional sausage casing and often sold coiled into a spiral. The sausages are then pan-fried, roasted, barbecued or grilled to a succulent golden brown. Buy them in Italian delis, but if unavailable, you could substitute any dense, coarse-textured, spicy Italian link sausages. Avoid soft, mild, rusk-softened sausages as they are totally unsuited to this dish. Luganega also makes a great addition to the barbecue.

3 tablespoons extra virgin olive oil

500 g luganega coarse-cut spicy pork spiral

750 g tinned Italian lentils, borlotti, cannellini or butter beans

4 garlic cloves, chopped

1 onion, grated

500 g wild rocket or fresh flat leaf parsley, washed and shaken dry

2 tablespoons dry vermouth or white wine

sea salt and freshly ground black pepper

SERVES 4

Heat half the olive oil in a heavy-based frying pan, add the sausage and fry over medium heat for 6–8 minutes or until very hot, browned and firm. Drain and discard the liquid from the pan. Keep the sausage hot over very low heat.

Meanwhile pour the lentils and their liquid into a saucepan and cook for 5 minutes or until very hot, then drain, discarding most of the liquid. Add salt, pepper, garlic, onion and the remaining oil and stir over medium heat.

Put the rocket in the pan with the hot sausage. Add the vermouth and cook briefly, covered, until the leaves are vividly green and wilted. Serve the sausages on lentils with the wilted greens alongside or on top.

Meatballs, or polpette, in tomato sauce are an integral part of Italian food culture. When cooked, it is common practice to serve the sauce with pasta as a first course, followed by the meatballs and maybe a vegetable. If you make the meatballs very small, you can serve them in sauce with spaghetti. The meat can also be cooked as a polpettone – rolled into one large piece, and simmered for a couple of hours. In this case, the sauce is certainly used to dress pasta first and the meat is sliced and served as a separate course.

pork and fennel meatballs in tomato sauce

450 g shoulder or leg of pork

225 g piece unsmoked gammon

225 g belly of pork

2 garlic cloves, crushed

2 tablespoon fennel seeds

a large pinch of chilli flakes

2 teaspoons sea salt

1 tablespoon sugar

2 tablespoons coarsely crushed black pepper

olive oil, for frying

50 ml dry white wine

400 g tinned chopped tomatoes

200 ml passata tomatoes

sea salt and freshly ground black pepper

SERVES 6

Trim the shoulder of pork, gammon and belly pork of any skin or connective tissue. Cut the meat into large chunks, then pass them through the coarse blade of an electric mincer or chop very finely with a large sharp knife or cleaver (do not use a food processor).

Put the meat in a large bowl, add the garlic, fennel seeds, chilli flakes, salt, sugar and pepper. Mix with clean hands or a large wooden spoon. At this stage, the sausage meat is ready to use, but you can cover the bowl and let it mature in the refrigerator overnight.

With dampened hands, shape into meatballs about the size of a walnut. To cook, heat 2 tablespoons of the olive oil in a frying pan and quickly brown the meatballs all over, in batches if necessary. Remove to a plate with a slotted spoon and add the wine. Deglaze the pan and let the wine bubble until there is only 1 tablespoon left. Add the canned tomatoes and passata, salt and pepper. Bring back to the boil, then return the meatballs to the sauce. Part-cover with a lid and simmer for 30–40 minutes, topping up with water if the sauce is becoming too dry. Serve as it is or dress pasta with the sauce as a first course and eat the meatballs as a course on their own (see recipe introduction).

This recipe, modelled on the more usual Veal Escalopes with Marsala, is easy to make with pork fillets, also called tenderloins, cut into small oval escalopes or scaloppine. Serve with side dishes such as buttered spinach or tiny roasted potatoes, and a glass of the same Marsala used in the sauce.

pork fillet with marsala

Cut the tenderloin crossways into 1-cm slices. Cut each slice almost through again, then open out and press flat with the heel of your palm. You should have about 24 flattened butterflied pieces or scaloppine.

Sift the flour, salt and ginger together onto a flat plate. Press 6 pieces of pork into this mixture until well coated on both sides.

Put half the butter and half the olive oil in a non-stick frying pan and heat until sizzling. Cook the almonds briefly until golden, then remove with a slotted spoon and set aside. Add 6 of the prepared scaloppine to the pan and cook for 2 minutes each side, pressing them down well, then use tongs to remove, and keep hot. Continue with a second batch of 6.

Add half the Marsala to the pan and stir to dissolve the sediment. Pour off into a bowl and keep it warm. Wash and dry the pan.

Using the remaining butter and oil, repeat the process until the second batch of pork is cooked. Keep hot in the same way.

Pour the remaining Marsala into the pan, then add the jellied meat stock or consommé. Scrape, stir and heat until well dissolved, then add the reserved warm pan sauce made earlier. Heat again until sticky and intensely flavoured. Return the pork to the pan and turn it in the hot sauce.

Serve 6 scaloppine per person, with a generous spoonful of the Marsala glaze and the almonds.

1½–2 pork tenderloins, about 750 g

100 g plain flour

1 teaspoon salt

1 teaspoon ground ginger or freshly grated nutmeg

50 g salted butter

2 tablespoons extra virgin olive oil

25 g blanched almonds, flaked or whole

100 ml sweet Marsala wine

2 tablespoons jellied veal or beef stock, or canned beef or chicken consommé

SERVES 4

osso buco with gremolata

The Italian name for this dish means 'bone with a hole'. For the last 1½ hours of cooking, you can cook this in the oven at 180°C (350°F) Gas 4 instead of on the stove, but make sure the casserole is flameproof. Gremolata is the traditional accompaniment for osso buco and should be made at the last minute to preserve its herby zing.

Dust the veal shins with flour. Heat the olive oil in a large saucepan, add the veal and fry over medium-low heat for a few minutes, until browned. Remove from the pan and set aside.

Add a little more oil to the pan if needed, heat and add the garlic, onions and celery. Cook for 5 minutes until soft but not browned. Add the tomato purée and tomatoes, mix well and add the wine, stock and salt and pepper to taste. Return the meat to the pan and gently bring to the boil. Cover with a lid and simmer gently for 1½ hours, adding a little more stock or wine from time to time if needed. Let cool, cover and chill.

When ready to serve, put the osso buco in a preheated oven at 180°C (350°F) Gas 4 until simmering, then continue cooking for 15 minutes or until heated right through.

Meanwhile, to make the gremolata, put the lemon zest, garlic and parsley into a bowl and stir well.

Remove the osso buco from the oven and serve topped with the gremolata and with mashed potato and green beans.

8 shins of veal with the marrow bone, 300 g each

4 tablespoons plain flour

4 tablespoons olive oil

3 garlic cloves, crushed and chopped

2 onions, chopped

4 celery stalks, chopped

1 tablespoon tomato purée

800 g tinned chopped tomatoes

200 ml dry white wine

300 ml vegetable stock

sea salt and freshly ground black pepper

GREMOLATA

finely grated zest of 3 lemons

3 garlic cloves, finely chopped

a large bunch of fresh flat leaf parsley, finely chopped

TO SERVE

mashed potato

steamed green beans

SERVES 8

Spanish fries are the traditional accompaniment for these succulent steaks and are extremely tasty due to the olive oil they are fried in. Deep-fried chilli peppers are another classic accompaniment, although they can be rather hot!

pan-grilled steaks with olive sauce

4 rib eye steaks, 2 cm thick

3 garlic cloves, crushed

3 tablespoons finely chopped fresh flat leaf parsley

5 tablespoons extra virgin olive oil

freshly squeezed juice of 1 lemon

sea salt and freshly ground black pepper

Spanish fries, to serve*

OLIVE SAUCE

4 tablespoons olive oil

1 tablespoon sherry vinegar

125 g mixed pitted green and black olives

2 garlic cloves, crushed

2 firm tomatoes, skinned, deseeded and finely chopped

sea salt and freshly ground black pepper

a ridged stove-top grill pan

SERVES 4

Put the steaks in a flat dish, sprinkle with the garlic, black pepper and half the parsley, pour over the olive oil and lemon juice, and rub in. Set aside for 2 hours or overnight in the refrigerator. Remove from the refrigerator 30 minutes before cooking and sprinkle with salt.

Meanwhile, to make the olive sauce, put the olive oil in a bowl and whisk in the sherry vinegar. Put the olives in a food processor and blend to chop into small, evenly sized bits (not a purée). Put in the bowl with the oil mixture, add the rest of the ingredients and season lightly with salt and pepper.

When ready to cook the steak, heat a ridged stove-top grill pan over high heat. When smoking, add the steaks and cook for 1½ minutes on each side for rare, 2 minutes for medium and 2½–3 minutes for well done. Alternatively, cook on the barbecue. Sprinkle with the rest of the parsley and serve with the sauce and pimientos de Padrón and Spanish fries, if liked.

*Note To make Spanish fries, cut 750 g potatoes, such as Belle de Fontenay, into 6-mm slices, then into 6-mm fingers. Rinse well in cold water to remove the starch, then pat dry on kitchen paper.

Fill a deep-fryer with pure olive oil to the manufacturer's recommended level and heat to 180°C (350°F). Working in batches, fry the potatoes until golden, then drain on kitchen paper and keep hot.

1 kg beef, such as shoulder or topside, cut into 1 cm thick slices

4 tablespoons extra virgin olive oil

4 garlic cloves, sliced

125 g thick-cut unsmoked bacon, cut in small dice, or bacon lardons, cubed

3 carrots, halved lengthways

12–16 baby onions, peeled

6 plum tomatoes, skinned, then thickly sliced

zest of 1 orange, removed in one piece

1 bunch of fresh herbs, such as parsley, thyme, bay leaf and rosemary, tied with string

60 g walnut halves

250 ml robust red wine

2 tablespoons Cognac or brandy

150 ml beef stock or water

15 cm square of pork or bacon rind (optional)

chopped flat leaf parsley, to serve

SERVES 4–6

This warming beef stew is a classic dish from the south of France. Rich with red wine, baby onions and orange zest, it can be served absolutely plain, or with accompaniments such as pasta, mashed potatoes or rice.

boeuf en daube

Cut the beef into 6-cm squares. Heat the olive oil in a large flameproof casserole and sauté the garlic, bacon, carrots and onions for about 4–5 minutes or until aromatic. Remove from the casserole. Put a layer of meat in the bottom of the casserole, then add half the sautéed vegetable mixture and a second layer of meat. Add the remaining vegetable mixture, the tomatoes, orange zest, bundle of herbs and walnuts.

Put the wine into a small saucepan and bring to the boil. Add the Cognac or brandy and warm for a few seconds, shaking the pan a little, to let the alcohol cook away. Pour the hot liquids over the meat with just enough stock so that it's barely covered. Put the pork rind, if using, on top.

Heat the casserole until simmering, then cover with foil and a lid and simmer gently for 2 hours or until the meat is fork tender and the juices rich and sticky.

The dish can also be cooked in the oven. Just bring to the boil over a high heat, reduce to a simmer, cover with foil, replace the lid and cook in the oven at 150°C (300°F) Gas 2 for 2½ hours or until very tender.

Remove and discard the rind: it will have given a velvety quality to the sauce. Sprinkle with parsley and serve hot.

meat roll simmered in tomato sauce

A traditional recipe from the Naples area, in which a lean piece of beef is rolled around a savoury stuffing and slowly cooked in a tomato and vegetable sauce. The sauce is usually served tossed with pasta as a first course, the meat served as the main course with just a little sauce, followed by a salad or a plate of green vegetables.

Soak the breadcrumbs in a little water. Soak the currants in lukewarm water for 15 minutes, then drain. Put the beef between 2 sheets of clingfilm and beat out with a meat mallet or rolling pin to flatten slightly, to about ½ cm thick. Season with salt and pepper.

Lightly squeeze out the soaked breadcrumbs and put in a bowl. Add 125 g of the chopped prosciutto, the parsley, garlic, marjoram and egg yolks, season with salt and pepper and mix well. Spread this mixture over the beef and sprinkle with the drained currants and the pine nuts. Roll up the beef, tucking in the sides, and tie up with fine string.

Heat the olive oil in the casserole dish on top of the stove, add the rolled beef and brown it all over. Transfer to a plate. Add the remaining prosciutto, the clove, onion, carrot and celery to the dish and cook for 10 minutes until the vegetables are soft. Stir in the tomato purée and 450 ml warm water.

Return the rolled beef to the dish and bring to the boil. Cover with a piece of greaseproof paper just large enough to fit inside your casserole dish. Cover with the lid, then transfer to a preheated oven at 180°C (350°F) Gas 4 for about 2 hours, adding a little extra water every now and then. When cooked, lift the beef out onto a warm plate, cover and set aside.

Pour the contents of the dish into a food processor and work to a purée. Reheat and taste for seasoning. To serve, slice the beef thickly and serve with a little sauce ladled over. Pass the remaining sauce around separately, or use for pasta.

125 g fresh breadcrumbs

1 tablespoon currants

1 slice of lean rump steak, about 500 g, about 1 cm thick

175 g prosciutto, finely chopped

6 tablespoons chopped fresh flat leaf parsley

1 garlic clove, finely chopped

½ teaspoon dried marjoram

2 egg yolks

1 tablespoon pine nuts

2 tablespoons olive oil

1 whole clove

1 small onion, finely chopped

1 small carrot, finely chopped

1 celery stalk, finely chopped

2 tablespoons tomato purée

sea salt and freshly ground black pepper

SERVES 4

vegetables

150 ml extra virgin olive oil

800 g or 3 medium aubergines, rinsed and halved lengthways

sea salt and freshly ground black pepper

STUFFING

2 onions, finely chopped

4 garlic cloves, finely chopped

1 teaspoon ground cumin

500 g ripe tomatoes, chopped

1 tablespoon dried oregano

½ teaspoon sugar

3 tablespoons chopped fresh flat leaf parsley

1 tablespoon tomato purée, diluted with 150 ml hot water

sea salt and freshly ground black pepper

SERVES 6

This is a dish full of summer flavours. It can be served hot as a main course or as part of a mixed meze as it is equally good served at room temperature. It derives its Turkish name, Imam Bayildi, from an old fable about the Turkish priest – the Imam – who fainted either from overindulging in this rich dish or from meanness because of the extravagant amount of olive oil used.

baked aubergines with garlic and tomatoes

Heat half the olive oil in a large frying pan, add 3 pieces of aubergine and shallow-fry, turning them over until light golden on both sides, 10–15 minutes. Remove and rest on kitchen paper. Repeat with the remaining 3 pieces. Arrange the pieces side by side in an ovenproof dish and season with salt and pepper.

To make the stuffing, heat the remaining olive oil in a saucepan, add the onions and sauté gently until they start to colour. Add the garlic and cumin, fry for 2–3 minutes, then add the tomatoes, oregano, salt, pepper, sugar and 150 ml water. Cover and cook for 15 minutes, stirring occasionally.

Stir in the parsley, then divide the stuffing into 6 equal portions. Pile each portion along the length of each aubergine half. Add the diluted tomato purée to the dish and cook in a preheated oven 190°C (375°F) Gas 5 for 45 minutes, basting the aubergines once during cooking. Serve hot or at room temperature.

ratatouille

Originally from Nice, ratatouille is one of those reliable recipes that just gets better as it matures. It can be served with many dishes, and also by itself with lots of crusty bread. Don't use green peppers as they are too bitter.

Cut the aubergines into large, bite-sized pieces, put them in a colander, sprinkle well with salt and let drain for 1 hour. Cut the peppers in half, remove the white membrane and seeds and slice the flesh into thick strips.

Heat the olive oil in a flameproof casserole and fry the onions, garlic and coriander seeds until soft and transparent, but not coloured. Add the wine and boil to reduce.

Meanwhile, rinse and drain the aubergines and dry on kitchen paper. Add the peppers and aubergines to the casserole and cook for about 10 minutes, stirring occasionally until softening around the edges, but not browning. Add the tomatoes, sugar and olives. Heat to simmering point, season well with salt and pepper, then half-cover and cook for about 25 minutes. Add the parsley, if using, and serve hot or cold.

2 aubergines

3 peppers (red, yellow or orange)

3 tablespoons olive oil

2 large onions, thinly sliced

2 garlic cloves, crushed

2 teaspoons finely crushed coriander seeds

5 tablespoons white wine

400 g tinned chopped tomatoes

1 teaspoon sugar

about 20 Greek-style dry-cured black olives

sea salt and freshly ground black pepper

parsley leaves, to serve (optional)

SERVES 6

This is a great dish for vegetarians and carnivores alike. Flavoured with fresh mint and sesame seeds and topped with spicy harissa sauce, the couscous goes well with any roast meat or vegetable dish. Morrocan Mint Tea (page 234) is delicious to drink after this dish.

sesame and mint couscous with winter vegetables

25 g unsalted butter

2 garlic cloves, crushed

1 tablespoon sweet Spanish paprika (page 65)

2 teaspoons cumin

½ teaspoon ground ginger

1 teaspoon sea salt

1 teaspoon freshly ground black pepper

2 bay leaves

2 tablespoons tomato purée

400 g tinned chopped tomatoes

2 whole fresh green chillies

2 large carrots, peeled and cut into wedges

2 large parsnips, peeled and cut into wedges

500 g potatoes, peeled and cut into 5-cm chunks

2 large courgettes, cut into wedges

200 g butternut squash or pumpkin, peeled, deseeded and cut into 5-cm chunks

2 tablespoons harissa paste mixed with 125 ml hot water, to serve

SESAME AND MINT COUSCOUS

375 g instant couscous

500 ml boiling water

125 g butter, cubed

4 tablespoons chopped fresh mint

3 tablespoons toasted sesame seeds

sea salt and freshly ground black pepper

SERVES 6

Melt the butter in a heavy casserole, add the garlic and cook for 1 minute over medium heat. Add the paprika, cumin, ginger, salt, pepper, bay leaves, tomato purée and tomatoes and stir well. Bring to the boil, then add the chillies, carrots and parsnips.

Pour in enough water to cover (about 400 ml), then return to the boil, part-cover with a lid and simmer gently for 20 minutes. Add the potatoes, courgettes and butternut squash, pushing them under the liquid, and cook for a further 20 minutes or until the potatoes are tender. Take care not to overcook the vegetables or they will disintegrate.

Meanwhile, make the sesame and mint couscous. Put the couscous in a bowl and pour the boiling water into a measuring jug, stir in the butter and mint, then pour evenly over the couscous. Cover tightly with clingfilm and let stand for 5 minutes.

Uncover the couscous and fluff up the grains with a fork. Stir in the sesame seeds, then taste and season well with salt and pepper. Pile the couscous onto a large serving platter, then make a hollow in the centre and heap the spicy vegetable stew into the middle. Serve immediately with the harissa paste mixture in a small bowl.

provençal vegetable tian

1 small aubergine, cut into 1-cm cubes

2 teaspoons salt

2 tablespoons extra virgin olive oil

2 tablespoons butter

4 garlic cloves, chopped

1 onion, sliced

4 spring onions or 1 baby leek, sliced

1 handful of spinach or Swiss chard, chopped

1 handful of baby asparagus or green beans, cut into 3-cm lengths

8 large eggs

250 ml crème fraîche or sour cream

75 g grated Parmesan, pecorino, or Gruyère cheese

SERVES 4

A tian is a shallow baking dish, often glazed earthenware. Like the word 'casserole', the name has also come to mean the food cooked in it. Tians usually contain vegetables and herbs and sometimes cheese and eggs, or even a little rice or petit salé bacon. It can be served in spoonfuls or in wedges, with bread or a salad.

Put the aubergine in a plastic or ceramic dish, sprinkle with the salt and set aside for 15 minutes or until all the other ingredients have been prepared.

Heat the olive oil and 1 tablespoon of the butter in a frying pan, add the garlic, onion, spring onions, spinach and asparagus and sauté over medium heat for 6–8 minutes, stirring constantly, until the vegetables are soft but still colourful. Remove with a slotted spoon.

Put the aubergine cubes in a colander and let drain – do not wash them. Pat them dry with kitchen paper, removing most of the salt. Add the remaining butter and the aubergine to the frying pan and sauté for 5 minutes.

Put the eggs, crème fraîche and Parmesan in a bowl and whisk with a fork.

Transfer the aubergine, vegetables and their juices and oil into a casserole dish, distributing them evenly. Pour the egg and cheese mixture over the top and bake in a preheated oven at 200°C (400°F) Gas 6 for 5 minutes. Reduce the heat to 180°C (350°F) Gas 4 for a further 20 minutes and cook until set and nicely browned.

Serve hot, warm or cool.

vegetables

Pastries are at the heart of Greek food and culture and each village and every island has its own indigenous versions. This sensational pie, known as spanakotyropitta, is the most common and most delicious kind. It can be served as a main course with rice or salad, or cut into small squares and served as a meze dish.

1 packet filo pastry, 400 g, thawed if frozen

150 g butter, melted

FILLING

500 g fresh leaf spinach, rinsed

4 tablespoons extra virgin olive oil

1 large onion, finely chopped

4–5 spring onions, trimmed and coarsely chopped

4 eggs

250 g feta cheese

90 g fresh dill, finely chopped

3–4 tablespoons finely chopped fresh flat leaf parsley

4 tablespoons milk

sea salt and freshly ground black pepper

a roasting tin, about 35 x 30 cm

MAKES ABOUT 12 PIECES

spinach and cheese pie

To make the filling, put the spinach in a large saucepan of water, cover and cook gently, stirring occasionally, for 5–6 minutes until wilted. Drain the spinach thoroughly in a colander. Wipe the saucepan dry, add the olive oil and sauté the onion and spring onions until translucent. Add the spinach, salt and pepper and sauté for 4–5 minutes. Let cool a little. Beat the eggs in a large bowl, crumble in the cheese, add the herbs, milk and spinach and mix well with a fork.

Unroll the pastry carefully – you will have an oblong stack of paper-thin sheets. Brush the roasting tin with the hot melted butter. Then butter sparingly the top sheet of pastry and lay it into the tin, folding any excess on one side (keep in mind that the pastry will shrink when cooked). Continue the same way folding the excess on alternate ends until you have used about half the pastry. Add the filling and spread it evenly. Fold the sides over it and start covering with the remaining pastry sheets, brushing each one with the melted butter. Try to be as neat as possible.

Finally, brush the top layer of pastry generously with butter. Using a sharp knife, score the top layers of pastry into diamond or square shapes – do it carefully to avoid spilling the filling. Using your fingertips, sprinkle a little cold water on top to stop the pastry curling.

Bake in a preheated oven at 190°C (375°F) Gas 5 for 50 minutes until golden on top. (It is nice to have it still a little moist in the centre.) Slice carefully all the way to the bottom sheets of pastry and serve hot or at room temperature.

peppers stuffed with caperberries

4 red or yellow peppers, quartered lengthways and deseeded

16 canned anchovy fillets, rinsed and drained

16 caperberries or 2 tablespoons capers, rinsed and drained

a small bunch of marjoram or oregano, chopped

2 tablespoons extra virgin olive oil

freshly ground black pepper

SERVES 4

Peppers are ubiquitous ingredients in Italian antipasti and respond well to grilling and roasting which develops the natural sugars. With salty anchovies and sharp pickled caperberries or capers, they really come into their own in this elegant dish from southern Italy.

Arrange the pepper quarters in a large roasting dish or tin.

Using scissors or a small knife, cut each anchovy fillet lengthways into 2 strips. Put 2 strips into each pepper segment. Add a caperberry or a share of the capers to each segment and sprinkle with the chopped herbs and olive oil.

Roast, uncovered, towards the top of a preheated oven at 180°C (350°F) Gas 4 for 20–30 minutes or until wrinkled, aromatic and beginning to char a little at the edges. Serve hot, warm or cool, sprinkled with black pepper.

This Spanish dish of summer or autumn vegetables roasted to sweetness is deceptively simple and its success depends on good olive oil and vegetables cooked in their skins for extra flavour. There are many Mediterranean variations and in some parts of France and Spain, you will find anchovy strips lining the pepper halves, or fragments of salt cod and sometimes capers, olives or even cubes of goats' cheese. Different herbs can be added just before serving and even a few drops of vinegar, but on the whole simplicity is best. Serve as an accompaniment or as a main dish with bread.

spanish roasted vegetables

Leave the stems on the peppers, but remove and discard the pith and seeds. Cut the onions almost in half crossways, leaving one side joined, as a hinge. Remove and discard the seeds and pith from the squash but leave otherwise intact.

Cut the unpeeled heads of garlic almost in half crossways, leaving a hinge of papery skin. Pour a teaspoon of the olive oil over the cut surfaces of the garlic, then put the bulbs back together again. Wrap up in foil, to make 2 packets.

Arrange all the prepared vegetables, including the aubergines, in a single layer in 1 or 2 roasting tins, cut sides uppermost. Sprinkle with 3-4 tablespoons of the oil.

Roast in a preheated oven at 250°C (475°F) Gas 9 for 35-40 minutes or until soft and fragrant. Transfer to a serving dish and sprinkle with black pepper and the herbs and remaining oil. Serve hot or warm.

2 red peppers, halved lengthways

2 yellow or orange peppers, halved lengthways

2 red onions, unpeeled

4 slices butternut squash or pumpkin, about 1.5 cm thick, deseeded if necessary, or 2 large courgettes, halved lengthways, scored with a fork

2 baby aubergines or 1 large, sliced lengthways and scored with a fork

2 whole garlic heads

6-8 tablespoons extra virgin olive oil

freshly ground black pepper

1 small handful of fresh herbs, such as parsley, oregano, mint and thyme

SERVES 4

artichokes provençal

Based on a Provençal dish, this is a delicious vegetable stew flavoured with lovage and thyme. Only a small amount of lovage is needed to give maximum flavour. If you've never tasted it, prepare to be smitten – it's a delightful herb, full of character, similar to celery in some ways. Baby artichokes are picked before the hairy choke has formed and can be cooked and eaten whole.

Squeeze the cut lemon halves into a bowl of cold water and add the lemon shells. Set aside to add the artichokes as they are prepared (the acidulated water will prevent them from discolouring).

To prepare the artichokes, remove about 3 layers of tough leaves from the outside, cut off the top 1 cm of the leaves and trim the stalks to about 3 cm. Using a vegetable peeler, peel the stalks. As you work, add the artichokes to the bowl of lemon water.

Heat 1 tablespoon of oil in the casserole, add the bacon and fry until crisp and golden. Transfer to a plate.

Add the remaining olive oil to a heavy flameproof casserole, then fry the whole shallots and garlic until golden. Drain the artichokes and add to the pan. Add the carrots and stir-fry for 2 minutes. Add the wine, bring to the boil and reduce for 2 minutes. Add the stock and simmer for 2 minutes, then add the lovage, thyme, salt and pepper.

Cover and cook in a preheated oven at 200°C (400°F) Gas 6 for 20 minutes until the artichokes are tender. Add the beans, return to the oven and heat through, uncovered, for 5 minutes. Serve with bread, boiled rice and salad.

1 lemon, halved

18–24 baby artichokes, depending on size

3 tablespoons extra virgin olive oil

200 g smoked bacon pieces (lardons)

300 g small shallots

3 garlic cloves, halved

4 carrots, halved lengthways and cut into fine strips

200 ml white wine

100 ml vegetable stock

2 young sprigs of lovage, or a few celery leaves

a large sprig of thyme

200 g cooked flageolet or cannellini beans

sea salt and freshly ground black pepper

TO SERVE

crusty bread

boiled rice

salad leaves

SERVES 6

The natural sugars in the vegetables are used in this Neapolitan dish to caramelize and combine with the vinegar, giving it its characteristic flavour. It is traditionally done quickly in a frying pan, but when cooking in quantity, it is easier to roast the vegetables in the oven.

sweet and sour carrots and courgettes with mint

2 medium courgettes

2 medium carrots

6 tablespoons extra virgin olive oil

a few sprigs of mint, plus extra to serve

2 tablespoons wine vinegar

sea salt and freshly ground black pepper

SERVES 4

Top and tail the courgettes and carrots and cut into chips the size of your little finger. Put half the olive oil in a bowl, add the carrots and toss to coat. Transfer the carrots to a roasting tin and cook in a preheated oven at 200°C (400°F) Gas 6 for 15 minutes.

Meanwhile, toss the courgettes in the remaining olive oil, then stir into the carrots when they have cooked for 15 minutes. Roast together for a further 10 minutes until tender and caramelized. Remove from the oven, season with salt and pepper, then add the mint and vinegar to the roasting tin, mixing well.

Set the tin over high heat on top of the stove and let it bubble for a few seconds to reduce the vinegar. Mix well. Serve hot or at room temperature with extra mint.

50 g dried currants or sultanas

12 saffron threads or 1 small packet (0.6 g) saffron powder

1 medium cauliflower, about 1 kg

4 tablespoons olive oil

1 onion, thinly sliced or finely chopped

2 garlic cloves, finely chopped

6 anchovy fillets in oil, rinsed and coarsely chopped, or 3 salted anchovies, boned, rinsed and chopped

sea salt and freshly ground black pepper

a handful of fresh basil leaves, to serve

BREADCRUMBS

4 tablespoons olive oil

1 whole garlic clove, peeled and lightly bruised to crack open

4 tablespoons dry or fresh breadcrumbs

SERVES 4

This dish originates from Sicily where there are several varieties of cauliflower, namely unblanched green cauliflower, blanched white cauliflower and a curious lime green variety with pointed florets - all of which can be cooked in the same way.

cauliflower with saffron and toasted breadcrumbs

To make the breadcrumbs, heat the olive oil in a frying pan, add the garlic clove, fry gently until lightly brown, then remove it from the pan. Stir in the breadcrumbs and cook over medium heat, stirring constantly, for 2 minutes until golden. Pour immediately into a sieve set over a bowl, to drain. Let cool.

Put the currants in a small bowl and pour over boiling water to cover. Let soak for 20 minutes. Put the saffron in a cup, add 3 tablespoons warm water and leave to infuse for 15–20 minutes. Remove the leaves and tough stalk from the cauliflower and divide the head into large florets. Cook for just 5 minutes in boiling salted water. Drain, reserving 150 ml of the cooking water.

Heat the olive oil in a deep frying pan and gently fry the onion and garlic for about 5 minutes until soft and golden. Stir in the anchovies and the drained currants and cook for 3 minutes until the anchovies dissolve. Add the saffron and its water, the drained cauliflower and the reserved cauliflower water. Stir well, then heat to a slow simmer. Season with pepper only. Part-cover and cook for 5 minutes until the cauliflower is tender. Serve sprinkled with the breadcrumbs and a few torn basil leaves.

whole onions
baked in their skins

In Sicily, onions are roasted in huge metal trays, then put on display outside vegetable shops. Sicilians love the sweetness of onions cooked like this. Normally the onions are simply squeezed out of their skins after roasting, but they also taste good finished off with a sweet and sour sauce.

Trim the root end of each onion so that they will stand up securely. Rub with olive oil. Cut a deep cross in the top of each one, slicing towards the base so that it is cut almost into quarters.

Pack the onions closely together in a flameproof casserole dish or roasting tin. Sprinkle with olive oil, salt and pepper. Bake in a preheated oven at 190°C (375°F) Gas 5 for 1-1¼ hours until tender in the centre.

Lift out the onions onto a serving dish, leaving the juices behind. Set the roasting tin over medium heat and add the wine, vinegar, sultanas, fennel seeds and capers. Scrape up any sediment and boil for a couple of minutes until reduced and syrupy.

Taste, add salt and pepper if necessary, then pour the sauce over the onions.

6 large white, red or purple onions

150 ml white wine

3 tablespoons red wine vinegar

2 tablespoons sultanas

1 teaspoon fennel seeds

1 tablespoon small salted capers, rinsed

sea salt and freshly ground black pepper

olive oil, for basting and serving

SERVES 6

With its lush intriguing taste, okra is the beloved vegetable of the Eastern Mediterranean. This vegetarian okra dish can be cooked well in advance and will wait happily at a meze table. The dried limes, which can be obtained from Arab or Indian stores, add an altogether new dimension to its sweet taste.

okra with dried limes

800 g fresh okra

150 ml extra virgin olive oil

1 large onion, sliced

1 teaspoon ground coriander

½ teaspoon ground allspice

700 g fresh tomatoes, sliced, or 400 g tinned tomatoes

2 dried limes (optional)

½ teaspoon sugar

2 tablespoons finely chopped fresh coriander

sea salt and freshly ground black pepper

SERVES 6

To prepare the okra, pare the conical tops with a sharp knife (similar to peeling potatoes). Put them in a bowl, cover with cold water briefly, then drain – handle with care.

Heat the olive oil in a wide saucepan, add the onion and sauté until light golden. Add the ground coriander and allspice, then when aromatic, add the tomatoes, dried limes, if using, sugar, salt and pepper. Cook for 10 minutes, pressing the limes with a spatula to extract their sour juices.

Add the okra and spread them evenly in the pan. Pour in enough hot water until they are almost immersed in the sauce.

Cook gently for about 30 minutes – shake the pan occasionally but don't stir as okra is fragile. Sprinkle the fresh coriander over the top and simmer for 5–10 minutes more. Serve warm or at room temperature.

250 g shelled broad beans,
fresh or frozen and thawed,
(650 g before shelling)

4 tablespoons olive oil

250 g spring onions,
coarsely chopped

300 ml vegetable stock
or water

4 tinned or frozen artichoke
hearts, quartered

250 g shelled peas,
fresh or frozen and thawed
(500 g before shelling)

a large pinch of sugar

2 tablespoons chopped
fresh mint

sea salt and freshly
ground black pepper

SERVES 4

This exquisite medley of green vegetables from western Sicily is one of the best ways to use sweet garden peas, broad beans and artichokes. Broad beans taste much better if popped out of their skins to reveal the bright green tender bean. This dish is often served as a soup, or you can add creamy ricotta to make a light lunch.

sicilian green vegetables

Bring a large saucepan of salted water to the boil, add the broad beans and boil for 1 minute. Drain and plunge them into a bowl of cold water to cool them quickly and set the colour. Nick the skin at the top of a bean and gently squeeze at the bottom to pop it out. Continue until all are done.

Heat the olive oil, add the spring onions and cook over gentle heat for a couple of minutes until they wilt and soften, but do not let brown. Add the stock and season well with salt and pepper. Bring to the boil, then reduce the heat and simmer for 5 minutes.

Add the peas and cook for a further 5 minutes, then gently stir in the beans and the artichoke hearts. Simmer for another 3–4 minutes. Remove from the heat and add sugar to taste, then stir in the mint. Let cool so the flavours will develop. Serve at room temperature.

1 kg fresh spinach

100 ml extra virgin olive oil

4 anchovy fillets in oil,
drained and chopped

3 tablespoons chopped fresh
flat leaf parsley

3 tablespoons dried currants or
small raisins, soaked in
warm water for 15 minutes

4 tablespoons pine nuts

freshly grated nutmeg

sea salt and freshly
ground black pepper

SERVES 4

This speciality of Genoa in Liguria uses anchovies as a way of adding saltiness, giving the earthy spinach a depth it would not have otherwise. The combination of salt (anchovies) and sweet (dried fruit), coupled with mild, creamy pine nuts in savoury dishes is common all over Italy.

spinach with anchovies and pine nuts

Tear the stems off the spinach, discard the stems and wash the leaves very well in plenty of cold water to remove any grit and sand. Shake dry in a colander or salad spinner, but leave some water clinging to the leaves.

Put the leaves in a covered saucepan and cook for a few minutes until they wilt. Drain in a colander but do not squeeze dry – you need large pieces of spinach.

Warm the olive oil in a large frying pan, add the chopped anchovies and parsley and stir for 2–3 minutes over medium heat until the anchovies dissolve. Add the spinach, drained currants and pine nuts. Add a good grating of nutmeg, taste, season with salt and pepper to taste and stir-fry for about 5 minutes until heated through, glossy and well mixed. Serve immediately.

pasta, bread and pizza

150 g salad potatoes, halved

350 g linguine or tagliatelle

150 g fine green beans

sea salt

PESTO ALLA GENOVESE

75 g pine nuts,
lightly toasted in a frying pan

3 garlic cloves, crushed
then chopped

25 g fresh basil leaves, torn

½ teaspoon coarse sea salt

25 g freshly grated
Parmesan cheese

25 g freshly grated
pecorino cheese

75 ml extra virgin olive oil

SERVES 4

Real Italian pesto is an exuberantly intense, rich paste of garlic, basil and cheese, given extra texture with pine nuts. Ligurians take pride in this culinary masterpiece: they say that the basil in their part of the Mediterranean has particular pungency. Aficionados suggest that half Parmesan and half pecorino cheeses will make the best pesto; others use only one type; some even add ricotta. Don't make the pesto too smooth: it should retain some texture and bite.

linguine with pesto alla genovese

To make the pesto, grind the pine nuts, garlic, basil and salt to a paste with a mortar and pestle or in a food processor, using the pulse button.

Keep stirring the paste with one hand (or have the machine still running) while you gradually add half the cheese, then half the olive oil. Repeat the process until you have a rich, stiff, vividly green paste or sauce.

Bring a large saucepan of water to the boil, then add a large pinch of salt. Add the potatoes and cook for 5 minutes. Add the pasta and cook until al dente, about 8 minutes more. After about 4 minutes, add the thin green beans. Drain and transfer to a large serving bowl. Add the pesto, toss well and serve immediately.

Note Fresh pesto is best used within hours, although it will keep for up to 1 week in the refrigerator if sealed in an airtight container.

sicilian spaghetti

Olive oil, garlic and assertive Mediterranean vegetables combine to produce this substantial pasta dish. The tiny tomato halves are oven-roasted and the cubes of aubergine salted, then sautéed, to intensify the tastes. The sauce is relatively dry and minimal and the dish is topped with handfuls of basil. Use whatever sturdy dry pasta is available: spaghetti, penne and rigatoni all taste excellent with this sauce.

Bring a large saucepan of salted water to the boil, ready to add the pasta when the vegetables are half cooked.

Put the aubergine cubes in a non-metal bowl, then add 1 teaspoon salt and set aside while you cook the tomatoes.

Pack the tomatoes, cut sides up, on an oven tray, sprinkle with the remaining salt and drizzle with 2 tablespoons of the olive oil. Roast in a preheated oven at 230°C (450°F) Gas 8 for 10 minutes or until wilted and aromatic.

Cook the pasta until al dente or according to the packet instructions.

Drain the aubergine and pat dry with kitchen paper. Heat 4 tablespoons of the olive oil in a non-stick frying pan. Add the aubergine and cook, stirring, over high heat until frizzled and soft, about 8 minutes. Add the roasted tomato halves, passata or juice, garlic and black pepper. Cook, stirring, for 2–3 minutes, then tear up most of the basil leaves and stir through. Test the pasta to make sure it is cooked, then drain.

Return the pasta to the saucepan and toss in the remaining olive oil. Divide between heated bowls, spoon over the sauce, add a few fresh basil leaves and serve.

1 aubergine, about 350 g, cut in 1-cm cubes

500 g mini plum tomatoes, halved and deseeded

125 ml extra virgin olive oil

400 g pasta, such as spaghettini or penne

125 ml passata tomatoes or tomato juice

2 garlic cloves, chopped

sea salt and freshly ground black pepper

leaves from 1 large bunch of fresh basil, to serve

SERVES 4

Resplendent with elegant ingredients such as lobster, prawns or crab, this pasta dish is a real treat for a special occasion. You can buy the lobster meat ready-prepared from a fishmonger or fish counter and it is deceptively easy to put together.

pappardelle with seafood sauce

Bring a large saucepan of salted water to the boil, ready to add the pasta once you have made the seafood sauce.

To make the sauce, heat the olive oil in a heavy-based frying pan. Add the lobster, prawn or crab meat, dill, chives and 1 tablespoon of the lemon juice, then season with salt and pepper. Heat briefly until the flavours blend well. Leave on a very low heat to keep warm.

Cook the pasta until al dente or according to the packet instructions. Drain, then tip into the seafood sauce. Toss gently with 2 wooden spoons, add the lemon zest and divide between 4 pasta bowls.

350 g pappardelle or tagliatelle

SEAFOOD SAUCE

180 ml extra virgin olive oil

450 g lobster meat, from 1 kg whole lobster, or prawn or crab meat

a bunch of fresh dill, chopped, about 40 g

a bunch of fresh chives, chopped, about 40 g

shredded zest and freshly squeezed juice of 1 lemon

sea salt and freshly ground black pepper

SERVES 4

The clams are the stars of this dish, but it's crucial that the sauce is smooth. If you only have tinned tomatoes, purée them with a hand blender or press them through a sieve before using. Delicious as this is, it's not an elegant meal to eat, so be prepared: tie your napkin firmly round your neck and use your fingers to pick the clams from their shells.

pasta con le vongole

2 tablespoons olive oil

2 garlic cloves, finely chopped

a sprig of fresh rosemary

500 ml tomato passata

½ teaspoon sugar

300 g dried pasta, such as spaghetti or linguine

1 kg fresh baby clams or cockles in shells

2 tablespoons chopped fresh flat leaf parsley

sea salt and freshly ground black pepper

SERVES 4

Heat the olive oil in a saucepan, add the garlic and rosemary and cook for 2 minutes. Add the passata and sugar, then season with salt and pepper to taste. Bring to the boil, cover and simmer for 30 minutes, then remove and discard the sprig of rosemary.

Meanwhile, bring a large saucepan of water to the boil. Add a pinch of salt, then add the pasta and cook until al dente, or according to the packet instructions.

While the pasta is cooking, put the clams and 2 tablespoons water into another large saucepan. Cover and cook over medium heat for 4–5 minutes, shaking the pan occasionally until all the shells have opened, and discarding any that remain closed.

Strain the clam cooking juices through a sieve into the tomato pan, to remove grit. When the clams are cool enough to handle, shell half of them and discard the empty shells. Add the shelled and unshelled clams to the tomato sauce and simmer for 3–4 minutes.

Drain the pasta and return it to the warm pan. Add the clams and parsley and toss to mix. Divide between 4 bowls and serve.

A classic, this famous dish was named, some say, after the charcoal burners or coalmen (carbonari) from Umbria and Lazio in Italy. Others believe it may have come about during World War II, with American soldiers bringing their wartime rations of bacon and eggs. Whatever the origins, it is delicious and very quick to make. The cheese, though optional, is frequently included, as is the cream.

spaghetti alla carbonara

Bring a large saucepan of water to the boil, then add a large pinch of salt. Add the spaghetti and cook until al dente or according to the packet instructions.

Put the pancetta in a heavy-based frying pan and cook until the fat runs and the pancetta is cooked but barely crisp. Add the garlic and remove from the heat.

Put the eggs, salt and pepper in a bowl and beat well, adding the cream, if using. Set aside.

As soon as the spaghetti is ready, drain it and put the bacon pan back over high heat. Toss in the hot pasta, then stir in the eggs and half of the Parmesan, if using, to make a creamy sauce. Remove the pan from the heat. Toss, using tongs, to mix everything well. Serve with the remaining Parmesan, if using, on top.

350 g spaghetti

150 g unsmoked or smoked pancetta (Italian bacon) or thinly-sliced rindless bacon, cut into 3-cm pieces

2 garlic cloves, crushed then chopped

3 large eggs

2 tablespoons thick cream (optional)

75 g freshly grated Parmesan cheese (optional)

sea salt and freshly ground black pepper

SERVES 4

Focaccia literally means 'a bread that was baked on the hearth', but it is easy to bake in conventional ovens. It is found in many different forms, and can be thin and crisp, thick and soft, round or square. Serve with olive oil, some balsamic vinegar for dipping and a handful of olives.

rosemary focaccia

750 g Italian '00' flour or plain white flour, plus extra for kneading

½ teaspoon fine sea salt

25 g fresh yeast or 1 sachet fast action dried yeast, 7 g

150 ml extra virgin olive oil

450 ml hand-hot water

coarse sea or crystal salt

sprigs of rosemary

a water spray

2 shallow cake tins, pie or pizza plates, 25 cm diameter, lightly oiled

MAKES 2 LOAVES

Sift the flour and salt into a large bowl and make a hollow in the centre. Crumble in the fresh yeast. For dried yeast, follow the packet instructions. Pour in 3 tablespoons of the olive oil, then rub in the yeast until the mixture resembles fine breadcrumbs. Pour in the hot water and mix with your hands until the dough comes together.

Transfer the dough to a floured surface, wash and dry your hands and knead for 10 minutes until smooth and elastic. The dough should be quite soft, but if too soft to handle, knead in more flour, 1 tablespoon at a time. Put the dough in a clean, oiled bowl, cover with a damp tea towel or clingfilm and let rise in a warm place until doubled in size, about 30 minutes–1½ hours.

Punch down the dough and cut in half. Put on a floured surface and shape each half into a round ball. Roll out into 2 circles, 25 cm diameter, and put in the tins. Cover with a damp tea towel or clingfilm and let rise for 30 minutes.

Remove the tea towel and, using your finger tips, make dimples all over the surface of the dough. They can be quite deep. Pour over the remaining oil and sprinkle generously with coarse salt. Cover again and let rise for 30 minutes. Spray with water, sprinkle the rosemary on top and bake in a preheated oven at 200°C (400°F) Gas 6 for 20–25 minutes. Transfer to a wire rack to cool. Eat the same day or freeze immediately.

Fougasse belongs to the same ancient family of breads as focaccie, the original hearth breads (page 191). In Provence, these flat, slashed 'ladder breads' (so called because of their shapes) are highly decorative and often flavoured with olives or herbs. Sweeter versions contain orange flower water and almonds and are associated with feast days.

fougasse

Put the olive oil, water and honey in a measuring jug and stir to dissolve. Put the flour, yeast and salt in a food processor. With the motor running, pour the liquid through the feed tube to form a dense dough. Stop, then repeat for 30 seconds more, to develop the gluten.

Transfer the dough to a large, oiled bowl, and cover with an oiled plastic bag. Leave in a warm place for at least 30 minutes or up to 2 hours until doubled in volume.

Punch down the risen dough, transfer to a well-floured work surface and knead for 5–8 minutes or until silky and smooth. Return to the bowl, cover and let rise again for 20 minutes or until doubled in size, then divide into 4. Squeeze, pat and knead 2 of the balls into ovals. Pat or roll out each oval on an oiled baking sheet, until it

is 3 times its original size, and about 1 cm thick. Make 2 rows of diagonal slashes in the dough, then open up the slashes to make larger holes. Tug out at the ends and sides if you'd like to open up the dough even more.

Brush the two breads all over with olive oil, then sprinkle with warm water. Add your choice of garlic, onion, olives, orange zest or orange flower water.

Bake each fougasse towards the top of a preheated oven at 220°C (425°F) Gas 7 for 15–20 minutes or until risen, crusty, but still chewy. Repeat with the other 2 portions of dough to make 4 small loaves.

Serve warm and eat with your fingers, pulling the bread into short lengths.

4 tablespoons extra virgin olive oil, plus extra for baking

450 ml lukewarm water

2 teaspoons honey or syrup (optional)

250 g malted wheatgrain flour (or 200 g malted wheatgrain flour plus 50 g buckwheat, triticale or spelt flour)

500 g strong white flour, plus extra for kneading

1 sachet fast-action dried yeast, 7 g

2 teaspoons sea salt

warm water, for baking

TOPPINGS

your choice of:

sliced garlic

onion rings

black olives, cut into strips

orange zest, thinly sliced

orange flower water

2 large baking sheets, oiled

MAKES 4 LOAVES

pissaladière

Packed with the flavours of Provence in southern France, this pizza-like bread is ideal picnic food. Soft, sweet onions scented with Provençal herbs are spread over a layer of tomato sauce, then topped with red pepper strips or sea-salty anchovies and black olives, all on a thin base.

3 tablespoons olive oil

1.5 kg mild onions, thinly sliced

3 garlic cloves, chopped

1 teaspoon dried herbes de Provence

TOMATO SAUCE

2 tablespoons olive oil

800 g tinned chopped tomatoes

3 tablespoons tomato purée

1 tablespoon capers, rinsed and drained

150 ml dry white wine

sea salt and freshly ground black pepper

YEAST DOUGH

7 g fresh yeast,
2 teaspoons dried yeast
or 1 teaspoon fast-action dried yeast

a pinch of sugar

150 g plain flour, plus extra for rolling

50 g unsalted butter, chilled and chopped

1 egg, beaten

a pinch of sea salt

TO FINISH

red pepper strips or about 10 anchovy fillets (optional)

olive oil, for drizzling

12–18 small black olives

a Swiss roll tin, 33 x 20 cm

SERVES 4–6

Heat the olive oil in a large saucepan, add the onions and garlic and stir well to coat with the oil. Add 1–2 tablespoons water, cover tightly and simmer over very low heat for about 1 hour until meltingly soft. Stir the onions from time to time to prevent them sticking, but don't let them colour. Add a little more water if they look dry. Stir in the herbs. Drain the mixture into a sieve over a bowl and reserve the liquid for the yeast dough.

To make the tomato sauce, heat the olive oil in a saucepan, add the tomatoes, tomato purée, capers, white wine, salt and pepper. Mix well and bring to the boil. Simmer, uncovered, for about 1 hour, stirring occasionally, until well reduced and very thick. Taste and adjust the seasoning. Set aside.

To make the yeast dough, cream the fresh yeast in a bowl with the sugar, then whisk in 3 tablespoons of the warmed reserved onion liquid. Leave for 10 minutes until frothy. For other yeasts, follow the packet instructions. Sift the flour into a bowl and rub in the butter. Make a hollow in the centre, add the egg, yeast mixture and a pinch of salt, and mix to a very soft dough – add more onion liquid if it seems dry. Knead in the bowl for 1–2 minutes until smooth. Put in an oiled bowl, cover with clingfilm and let rise for 1 hour or until doubled in size.

Knock back the dough, knead lightly, then roll out on a lightly floured surface. Use to line the tin, pushing the dough well up the edges. Spread the reduced tomato sauce thinly over the dough base. Cover with the onions. Arrange the red pepper strips, if using, in a lattice on top of the onions. Alternatively, cut the anchovy fillets in half lengthways and use them instead. Drizzle with a little olive oil and bake in a preheated oven at 190°C (375°F) Gas 5 for about 1 hour until the pastry is golden and crisp. Arrange the olives on top and serve warm or cold.

Something like a double-thickness, well-stuffed pizza, this ancient recipe is really a kind of substantial double-crust pie. Vary ingredients as you like, though these are fairly typical for a Sicilian recipe – food from this island is often packed with intense flavours.

sicilian schiacciata

Put the flour, sugar, salt and yeast into a food processor. Pulse a few times to mix and sift.

Put the warm water, egg and olive oil in a bowl or jug and whisk well. With the machine running, add the mixture to the processor through the feed tube. The dough will form, clump, then gather in a mass. Remove to a well-floured work surface, sprinkle with extra flour and knead the dough for 2–3 minutes or until smooth and silky.

Put the ball of dough into a lightly oiled bowl and enclose in a large plastic bag. Leave in a warm place until doubled in size, about 1 hour. Remove from the bowl and punch down the dough. Cut it in half, then roll, pat and stretch each piece to about 30 cm diameter.

Stretch one of the rounds to about 2 cm more and slide onto a heavy baking tray. Sprinkle it with the cheese, the anchovies and their oil, the prosciutto, onions, tomatoes, olives and chilli. Wet your fingers and sprinkle some drops of water all over and around the edges.

Press the remaining round of dough on top. Push down with your knuckles to seal, then use a fork to press and prick all over in a decorative pattern. Press your fingertips all over to make deep indentations. Wet both hands and sprinkle more water on top, then sprinkle with the olive oil, salt, pepper and oregano. Let rise in a warm place for about 1 hour or almost doubled in size.

Bake in a preheated oven at 250°C (475°F) Gas 9 for 15 minutes, then reduce the heat to 200°C (400°F) Gas 6 and cook for a further 25–30 minutes or until crisp, golden and fragrant – it should sound hollow when you tap the bottom of the loaf with your knuckles.

Eat hot or warm in squares, segments or pulled into chunks.

500 g strong white bread flour, plus extra for shaping

2 tablespoons sugar

1½ teaspoons salt

1 sachet fast-action dried yeast, 7 g

300 ml lukewarm water

1 large egg, beaten

2 tablespoons extra virgin olive oil

FILLING

150 g caciocavallo or scamorza cheese (smoked mozzarella), chopped or sliced

50 g tinned anchovies with their oil

4 slices (about 80 g) prosciutto, speck or other cured Italian ham, pulled into pieces

2 red or white onions, sliced finely into rings, blanched in boiling water and drained

8 sun-dried tomatoes in oil, chopped

16 green or black olives, pitted

1–1½ teaspoons crumbled dried red chilli

1 tablespoon extra virgin olive oil

1 teaspoon sea salt

2 teaspoons cracked black peppercorns

1 teaspoon dried oregano or 2 teaspoons fresh, chopped oregano

SERVES 4–6

250 g fine Italian semolina flour (farina di semola)

7 g fresh yeast, 2 teaspoons dried yeast or 1 teaspoon fast-action dried yeast

1 tablespoon freshly squeezed lemon juice

1 tablespoon olive oil

a pinch of sea salt

about 300 ml warm water

SALSA PIZZAIOLA

8 tablespoons olive oil

2 garlic cloves, chopped

1 teaspoon dried oregano

800 g fresh tomatoes, skinned and coarsely chopped or 800 g tinned chopped tomatoes

sea salt and freshly ground black pepper

PIZZA TOPPING

250 g fresh mozzarella cheese, thinly sliced

a large handful of fresh basil leaves

olive oil, for drizzling

sea salt and freshly ground black pepper

a 'testa' or terracotta bakestone or 2 large heavy baking sheets

MAKES 2 PIZZAS

This classic pizza was originally made in honour of Queen Margherita of Naples, symbolizing the Italian national flag, with its green, white and red topping.

pizza alla margherita

Put the bakestone or baking sheets in the oven and preheat to 220°C (425°F) Gas 7.

To make the dough, put the semolina flour in a bowl and crumble the fresh yeast into the flour. For other yeasts, follow the packet instructions. Add the lemon juice, olive oil and a generous pinch of salt, then add enough warm water to form a very soft dough. Transfer to a floured surface and knead for 10 minutes or until smooth and elastic. Put the dough in a clean, oiled bowl (or an oiled plastic bag), cover and let rise until doubled in size (about 1 hour).

Meanwhile make the salsa pizzaiola. Put the olive oil in a large shallow pan and heat almost to smoking point. Standing back (it will splutter if it's at the right temperature), add the garlic, oregano and tomatoes. Cook over a fierce heat for 5–8 minutes or until thick and glossy. Season with salt and pepper.

Cut the dough in half and knead each half into a round. Pat or roll the rounds into 25-cm circles, keeping the bases well floured. Transfer the pizzas onto baking sheets lined with non-stick baking parchment. Spread each one lightly with salsa pizzaiola, cover with sliced mozzarella and season with salt and pepper. Let rise in a warm place for 10 minutes, then open the oven door, and slide paper and pizza onto the hot bakestone or baking sheets. If you are brave, try to shoot them into the oven so that they leave the paper behind – this takes practice.

Bake for 18–20 minutes, until the crust is golden and the cheese melted but still white. Remove from the oven, sprinkle with basil leaves and drizzle with olive oil, then eat immediately.

15 g fresh yeast, 1 tablespoon dried active yeast, or 1 sachet fast-action dried yeast, 7 g

a pinch of sugar

250 ml lukewarm water

350 g plain white flour, plus extra, for dusting

1 tablespoon olive oil, plus extra for brushing

a pinch of salt

FILLING

100 g cubed melting cheese, such as mozzarella

100 g cubed salami, ham or cooked sausage

50 g cooked chopped spinach

4 sun-dried tomatoes in oil, chopped

3–4 tablespoons Salsa Pizzaiola (page 198)

2–3 tablespoons chopped mixed herbs

sea salt and freshly ground black pepper

SERVES 2

Italians are thrifty, and a really delicious double-crust pizza can be made with a carefully chosen mixture of leftovers. There must be cheese to keep it moist, but you can add anchovies, cooked meat sauce, capers or olives – whatever you like, as long as their flavours suit each other.

pizza rustica

To make the dough, put the fresh yeast and sugar in a medium bowl and beat until creamy. Whisk in the warm water and leave for 10 minutes until frothy. For other yeasts, follow the packet instructions.

Sift the flour into a large bowl and make a hollow in the centre. Pour in the yeast mixture, olive oil and a large pinch of salt. Mix with a round-bladed knife, then your hands, until the dough comes together. Transfer to a floured surface, wash and dry your hands and knead for 10 minutes until smooth and elastic. The dough should be quite soft, but if too soft to handle, add more flour, 1 tablespoon at a time. Put the dough in a clean, oiled bowl, cover with a damp tea towel or clingfilm and let rise until doubled in size – about 1 hour.

To make the filling, put the mozzarella, salami, spinach, sun-dried tomatoes, salsa pizzaiola and mixed herbs in a bowl and season with salt and pepper.

Roll out the dough to a large circle, making sure it is well floured so it doesn't stick. Pile the filling onto one half of the dough, avoiding the edges. Flip over the other half to cover, press the edges together to seal, then twist and crimp. Slide onto a floured baking sheet and brush lightly with olive oil. Make a slash in the top to prevent it exploding when cooking.

Bake in a preheated oven at 220°C (425°F) Gas 7 for about 25 minutes until golden and firm. Remove from the oven, set aside for 5 minutes, then serve.

turkish pizza turnover

350 g strong white flour, plus
extra for kneading

1½ teaspoons fast action
dried yeast

1½ teaspoons sea salt

1 tablespoon extra virgin
olive oil

150–175 ml lukewarm water

CHEESE AND SPINACH FILLING

500 g spinach leaves

1 tablespoon extra virgin
olive oil

1 small onion, finely chopped

2 garlic cloves, crushed

125 g feta cheese, crumbled

2 tablespoons grated
Parmesan cheese

2 tablespoons
mascarpone cheese

a little freshly grated nutmeg

freshly ground black pepper

*a flat griddle or large
heavy-based frying pan*

SERVES 4

*These turnovers are similar to the Italian 'calzone' or stuffed pizza.
They are sold in Turkish markets, cut into thin strips. They can also be
cooked on a barbecue with a flat plate – brush the bread with olive
oil and cook for 5 minutes, turning once.*

Sift the flour into the bowl of an electric mixer* with dough hook attached. Stir
in the yeast and salt. Add the olive oil and warm water and work until the dough
is smooth and elastic.

Meanwhile, to make the filling, discard any thick spinach stalks, then wash the
leaves in a colander. Drain, transfer to a large saucepan and heat gently for
2–3 minutes until the leaves have wilted. Rinse under cold water, drain completely
and squeeze out as much water as possible. Finely chop the spinach and set aside.

Heat the olive oil in a frying pan, add the onion and garlic and fry gently for
5 minutes until very soft and lightly golden. Stir in the spinach, cheeses, nutmeg
and pepper, then remove from the heat.

Transfer the dough back onto a floured surface and knead it gently. Divide the
dough into 4 equal pieces and roll out each piece to a rectangle 20 x 40 cm
(it will be very thin). Spread a quarter of the spinach mixture over half the
dough, fold over and seal the edges. Repeat with the other pieces of dough to
make 4 turnovers.

Cook on a flat griddle or large, heavy-based frying pan. Serve hot.

*Note If you don't have an electric mixer, use a food processor with the plastic
blade attachment, or make by hand in a large mixing bowl. Gradually work the
mixture together with your hands to form a soft dough, then turn out onto
a lightly floured surface and knead for 8–10 minutes until the dough becomes
smooth and elastic.

sweet things and drinks

150 ml single cream and milk, mixed half and half

zest of 1 lemon, cut into 8 long strips, bruised

50 g caster sugar

3 large eggs

2 teaspoons vanilla extract

4 tablespoons caster sugar, to glaze

4 shallow heatproof dishes, 80 ml each

a baking tin

a cook's blowtorch (optional)

SERVES 4

These superb caramelized egg custards scented with strips of lemon zest are one of the joys of Spain. This version is from Catalonia. Often they are made in small, shallow, individual earthenware dishes, called cazuelas (page 33). Catalonia once briefly included Sicily, Sardinia and Naples, so there are interesting culinary influences from these neighbouring cuisines. You can caramelize the sugar under a hot grill or use a blowtorch if you have one. Be sure to have the heat source very hot – you do not want to damage, melt or toughen the delicate custard beneath by undue browning.

spanish flans

Put the cream and milk, and 4 of the strips of lemon zest in a saucepan and heat almost to boiling (this is called scalding). Put the pan in a bowl of iced water to cool it quickly. Put the sugar, eggs and vanilla in a bowl and whisk until well blended, trying to avoid making froth. Stir in the cooled scalded cream.

Pour the custard mixture into the 4 dishes, then tuck one of the remaining strips of lemon zest into each custard.

Set the dishes in a baking tin and add enough boiling water to come halfway up the sides of the dishes. Bake towards the top of a preheated oven at 150°C (300°F) Gas 2 for 20 minutes or until very gently set and wobbly. Remove the baking tin from the oven, then remove the dishes from the tin.

To glaze the custards, sprinkle the sugar evenly over each one. Preheat an overhead grill to very hot, leaving space for the pots to be 3 cm from the heat. Alternatively, turn on a blowtorch. Grill or blowtorch the custards until a fine layer of caramel forms on top. Serve, preferably at room temperature, within 2 hours.

The secret of a great panna cotta is in the wobble. Panna cotta means 'cooked or scalded cream' and is said to have originated in Piedmont or Lombardy, where the cream and milk are very rich.

500 ml double cream

300 ml milk

1 vanilla pod, split

50 g caster sugar

3 sheets leaf gelatine or
3 teaspoons powdered gelatine

CANDIED ORANGE ZEST

2 oranges

50 g caster sugar

6 moulds, about 125 ml each

SERVES 6

panna cotta with candied orange zest

To make the panna cotta, put the cream and milk, split vanilla pod and sugar in a saucepan and bring to the boil. Crumble or sprinkle the gelatine into the cream and stir until dissolved. Cool, then chill in the refrigerator until it just begins to thicken. At this stage, stir the cream briskly to distribute the vanilla seeds, then remove the vanilla pod. (Rinse and dry and keep in the sugar jar.) Pour into the moulds, set on a tray and refrigerate for at least 5 hours or until set.

Remove the zest from the oranges with a sharp potato peeler (removing any bitter white pith with a knife afterwards). Cut the zest into long, fine shreds. Bring a small saucepan of water to the boil and blanch the shreds for 1 minute. Drain, then refresh in cold water.

Put the sugar and 100 ml water in a small saucepan and stir until dissolved. Add the orange shreds and bring to a rolling boil. Boil for 2–3 minutes, then strain the shreds through a sieve and transfer to a plate to cool. Before they cool too much, separate them out a little so they don't stick together.

To serve, press the top of the panna cotta and gently pull away from the edge of the mould (this breaks the airlock). Carefully invert onto a small cold plate. (Give the mould a good shake and the panna cotta should drop out.) If it still won't turn out, dip very briefly into warm water, then invert onto the plate and lift off. Top with the orange shreds and a spoonful of syrup.

Strawberries, when freshly picked and at the height of their summery sweetness, are a joy: they should be simply eaten on their own. At other times strawberries may need a little assistance to coax out their full potential, as in this recipe.

sugared strawberries

To make the spiced sugar, put the cinnamon, peppercorns, sugar and lemon zest in an electric coffee grinder or small spice grinder. Grind in continuous bursts to make a powdery spiced mixture.

Put the strawberries in a bowl and spoon half the mixture on top, gently stirring and mixing to encourage the juices to run. Leave for 10 minutes. Meanwhile, press the ricotta through a sieve into a bowl with the back of a spoon. Mix in the liqueur, the remaining spiced sugar and the vinegar to form a cream.

To serve, put spoonfuls of the creamy mixture in small, stemmed glasses or glass or china dishes, then pile the berries on top and sprinkle them with a few extra drops of liqueur.

2 pints ripe, red strawberries, washed, dried, hulled and halved

250 g fresh ricotta cheese

1 tablespoon Amaretto liqueur, plus extra to serve

½ teaspoon balsamic vinegar

SPICED SUGAR

½ stick of cinnamon, crushed

6 peppercorns, crushed

6 tablespoons sugar

8-cm strip of lemon zest

SERVES 4

This ice cream really does taste like an Italian gelato. It is silky smooth and heavenly, served in a glass coppa with delicious warmed Amarena cherries. Amarena cherries are sold in pretty white and blue glass jars – a great souvenir of a holiday in Italy, but they are less expensive bought in tins from a delicatessen.

vanilla gelato with hot cherry sauce

1 vanilla pod, split

1.1 litres full cream milk

2 tablespoons dried skimmed milk powder

4 tablespoons cornflour or wheat starch

275 g caster sugar

1 teaspoon real vanilla essence

370 g tinned Italian Amarena cherries in syrup

2 tablespoons maraschino or kirsch

an ice cream maker (optional)

SERVES 6

Put the split vanilla pod in a saucepan with 900 ml of the milk, then whisk in the milk powder. Bring to boiling point, turn off the heat and leave to infuse for 20 minutes.

Remove the vanilla pod and scrape out the seeds into the milk. Whisk the seeds through the milk. Wash and dry the pod and store in the sugar jar.

Dissolve the cornflour in the remaining milk, then pour into the hot milk and add the sugar. Set over the heat again and bring to the boil, stirring constantly until thickened. Cover the surface with clingfilm and let cool to room temperature. Stir in the vanilla essence. Chill, then churn in an ice cream maker for 20–25 minutes or until set.

Alternatively, pour into a shallow freezer tray and freeze until frozen around the edges. Mash well with a fork. When it is half-frozen again, blend in a food processor until creamy, then cover and freeze until firm. Let soften in the refrigerator for 20 minutes before serving.

When ready to serve, put the cherries, their syrup and the liqueur in a saucepan and heat gently. Serve the ice cream in large scoops with the sauce trickled over it.

bitter chocolate and hazelnut gelato

75 g blanched hazelnuts, finely chopped

175 g vanilla sugar or caster sugar

150 ml whole milk

250 g dark chocolate, with at least 70% cocoa solids, broken in pieces

1 tablespoon glucose syrup or corn syrup

1 tablespoon chocolate or hazelnut liqueur or dark rum

400 ml double cream

crisp wafers or biscuits, to serve (optional)

an electric ice cream maker or a 1-litre freezerproof container

SERVES 4–6

Italian and French gelaterias offer splendid, often simple flavour combinations when it comes to ice cream. Chocolate and nuts are particularly delicious, especially if the chocolate is of the high-quality, bitter-sweet type. If you have a pestle and mortar, try to pound the nuts and sugar to a very smooth texture – otherwise use an electric coffee grinder or spice grinder in short bursts.

Put the chopped hazelnuts in a dry frying pan and dry-cook over medium heat, stirring constantly until they darken and smell toasty, about 2–3 minutes (take care, because they burn easily). Pour out onto a plate and let cool.

Put the toasted hazelnuts and 4 tablespoons of the sugar in a small electric spice grinder or coffee grinder. Grind in brief bursts, to a smooth, speckly powder.

Put the milk, chocolate and remaining sugar in a saucepan over very gentle heat. Cook until the chocolate melts, stirring constantly, then add the glucose syrup and ground sugar and nuts. Remove from the heat, put the pan into a bowl of iced water and let cool. Stir in the liqueur and cream and cool again.

Pour the prepared mixture into the ice cream maker and churn for 20–25 minutes or until set. Alternatively, freeze in the container, covered, for 6 hours, beating and whisking it once, after 3 hours.

Serve in scoops with wafers or biscuits, if using.

A beautiful, pink, exotic sorbetto from Sicily, delicately perfumed with a hint of cinnamon or jasmine flower water. Just for fun, the chocolate chips represent the black watermelon seeds, but they do add a nice crunchy texture. You won't need a whole watermelon for this recipe, so keep the rest to eat on its own or make into a fruit salad.

watermelon sorbet with chocolate chip seeds

750 g red watermelon flesh, cut into cubes

150 g caster sugar (or a bit less if the melon is very sweet)

1 small cinnamon stick

freshly squeezed juice of 2 ripe lemons

a little pink food colouring, if necessary

75 g plain chocolate chips

an ice cream maker or a shallow freezer tray, 2 cm deep

SERVES 4–6

Remove the seeds from the melon with the tip of a small knife. Put the flesh in a food processor and purée until smooth. With the machine running, pour in the sugar and blend for 30 seconds.

Pour the melon mixture into a saucepan and add the cinnamon stick. Slowly bring to the boil, stirring all the time to dissolve the sugar completely, then turn down the heat to a bare simmer for 1 minute. Remove from the heat, add the lemon juice and a few drops of pink food colouring if necessary.

Let cool. When cold, remove the cinnamon stick and chill the mixture in the refrigerator for at least 1 hour (or overnight – this makes freezing quicker).

Transfer to an ice cream maker and freeze according to the manufacturer's instructions. Stir in the chocolate chips when the sorbetto is still soft. Transfer to a chilled freezer container, cover and freeze until firm. Let soften in the refrigerator for 20 minutes before serving.

Alternatively, pour into a shallow freezer tray and freeze until the sorbetto is frozen around the edges. Mash well with a fork. When it is half frozen again, blend in a food processor until creamy, stir in the chocolate chips, then cover and freeze until firm. Let soften in the refrigerator for 20 minutes before serving.

This Sicilian granita is superbly refreshing. The blanched almonds are blended with sugar and iced water to form a sweet milk-like liquid and the Amaretto liqueur adds extra almond flavour.

almond milk granita, laced with amaretto

Put the almonds and sugar in a food processor and grind as finely as you can. Add 500 ml iced water and process for 2–3 minutes until very milky.

Pour this mixture into the blender with the remaining 500 ml iced water (you may have to do this in 2 batches). Blend on high speed for 2–3 minutes to grind the almonds as finely as possible. Pour into a bowl or jug, cover and transfer to the refrigerator for several hours or overnight for the almonds to settle. Strain the settled almond milk from the sediment through a fine sieve or muslin into the freezer tray. Stir in the Amaretto.

Cover and freeze for about 30 minutes, until the edges start to freeze. Scrape the frozen edges into the centre with a fork and mash the mixture evenly. Repeat every 30 minutes until it forms a mound of shimmering ice crystals. Serve in chilled glasses with your prettiest silver spoons.

100 g blanched almonds

100 g caster sugar

1 litre iced water

3 tablespoons Amaretto liqueur

a shallow freezer tray, 2 cm deep

SERVES 8

Lemon tart – wobbly, sharp, creamy, but acidic – is an outrageously delicious dish. In France, a tarte au citron is often a slim, very elegant offering, not heavily filled. The ideal is to make it a few hours before you intend to eat it, then serve it warm or cool. Some ice-cold scoops of thick, sharp crème fraîche are the perfect accompaniment. Serve with a small glass of citrus liqueur, dark rum or brandy.

classic lemon tart

6 tablespoons icing sugar, sifted

175 g butter, at
room temperature

2 large egg yolks

2 tablespoons iced water

250 g plain flour, sifted

LEMON FILLING

4 large eggs

150 g caster sugar

2 tablespoons grated lemon
zest from 2–3 lemons

125 ml freshly squeezed
lemon juice

100 ml crème fraîche or double
cream, plus extra to serve

*a loose-bottomed round tart tin,
20-cm diameter and 3 cm deep,
set on a baking sheet*

*greaseproof paper and
baking beans*

SERVES 4

To make the dough, set aside 2 tablespoons of the icing sugar and put the remainder in the bowl of an electric mixer. Add the butter and beat until creamy, soft and white. Add the egg yolks one at a time and continue beating until well mixed. Trickle in half the iced water, then add the flour. Beat on a lower speed, adding the remaining water until the dough gathers into a soft ball. Wrap in clingfilm and chill for 40–60 minutes.

Transfer the dough to a floured work surface and roll out to 5 mm thick. Use it to line the tart tin. Gently push the dough into the corners. Cut off the excess dough. Chill for a further 20 minutes or until very firm.

Prick the dough all over with a fork, line with greaseproof paper, fill with baking beans, and bake blind in a preheated oven at 180°C (350°F) Gas 4 for 15 minutes. Remove the paper and the beans. Let the pastry rest for 5 minutes, then bake again for 10 minutes or until pale golden.

To make the filling, put the eggs, sugar and half the lemon zest in a bowl and beat well for 2 minutes with a electric whisk. Stir in the lemon juice and crème fraîche, then pour the mixture into the pastry case. Bake at 120°C (250°F) Gas ½ for 35 minutes, or until the filling is barely set.

While the tart cooks, put the remaining lemon zest in a sieve, pour over boiling water, then refresh under cold running water. Put the zest, the reserved 2 tablespoons icing sugar and 4 tablespoons water in a saucepan over low heat. Cook gently until the zest looks syrupy. Sprinkle the zest over the cooked tart. Serve hot or warm, with additional spoonfuls of crème fraîche.

You'll find simple tarts made with seasonal fruit all over Italy. The ricotta makes a lovely light cheesecake with a slightly grainy texture. Be sure to try this only with fresh figs – dried are not the same. If figs aren't in season, all sorts of other fruits can be used to top the tart.

caramelized fig tart

75 g butter, softened

75 g sugar

3 egg yolks

½ teaspoon pure vanilla extract

175 g plain flour, plus extra for dusting

1 teaspoon salt

1 egg yolk, beaten, for brushing

FIG FILLING

225 g fresh ricotta cheese

125 g butter, softened

125 g caster sugar or vanilla sugar

2 eggs

8–10 ripe black figs (depending on size), cut in halves or quarters

redcurrant jelly

a loose-bottomed round tart tin, 20 cm diameter

baking beans

SERVES 6

To make the pastry, put the butter, sugar, the 3 egg yolks and vanilla in a food processor and blend until smooth.

Sift the flour and salt onto a sheet of greaseproof paper. Shoot the flour into the food processor and blend until just mixed.

Transfer to a floured work surface and knead gently until smooth. Form into a ball, flatten and wrap in clingfilm. Chill for at least 30 minutes.

To make the filling, put the ricotta, butter and sugar in a bowl and beat until smooth. Put the 2 eggs in another bowl, beat well, then gradually beat them into the cheese mixture. Set aside.

Roll out the pastry thinly and use to line the tart tin. Prick the base all over with a fork, then chill or freeze for 15 minutes. Line with aluminium foil and baking beans, set on a baking sheet and bake blind in the centre of a preheated oven at 190°C (375°F) Gas 5 for 10–12 minutes. Remove the foil and beans, brush with the beaten egg yolk and cook for a further 5 minutes until golden.

Remove the pastry case from the oven, let it cool slightly, then pour the filling into it and bake for a further 25–30 minutes until risen and brown.

Remove from the oven and let cool in the tin for 10 minutes, then transfer to a wire rack to cool completely. Arrange the figs, cut side up, on top of the tart. Warm the redcurrant jelly and lightly brush the figs with it.

Protect the pastry edges with foil to prevent over-browning. Preheat the grill and set the tart close to the heat. Grill quickly until the figs are just browning, then serve immediately.

greek honey, walnut and brandy cake

125 ml extra virgin olive oil

100 g caster sugar

2 eggs

200 g walnut pieces

185 g self-raising flour, sieved

¼ teaspoon salt

125 ml strained plain Greek yoghurt or thick-set yoghurt

2 tablespoons brandy, preferably Greek Metaxa

2 tablespoons clear honey

a loose-based round cake tin, 20 cm diameter, lightly oiled and base-lined

SERVES 8–12

Halvas is a classic semolina and almond cake-like pudding. Greeks know its golden formula – 1,2,3,4 – by heart: 1 cup olive oil, 2 cups semolina, 3 cups sugar and 4 cups water (a cup is 250 ml). This pudding can be elaborated into a proper baked cake like this one, using olive oil, not butter. Serve it with a blob of thick Greek yoghurt and a glass of Greek Metaxa brandy for a real treat.

Put the olive oil, sugar and eggs in a large bowl and whisk with an electric beater until light and fluffy. Reserve a handful of the walnut pieces for decoration and chop the remainder with a knife or food processor in brief bursts until fine, but not mealy.

Add to the bowl, together with the flour, salt and yoghurt. Using broad strokes, mix the batter with a wooden spoon until smooth and even. Do not overmix.

Spoon the mixture into the prepared cake tin and smooth flat on top. Scatter with the reserved nuts.

Bake towards the top of a preheated oven at 175°C (325°F) Gas 3 for 40 minutes.

Test the centre – a skewer inserted into the centre should come out clean. Listen for a popping, bubbling sound too.

Put the brandy and honey in a small bowl and stir until dissolved. Trickle the mixture over the top of the cake, then let cool in the tin for 20 minutes.

Remove the cake, still on its loose metal base, and cool on a wire rack for 10 minutes. Remove the base, peel off the paper and serve warm or cold. The cake will keep in an airtight container for 4 days.

This Mediterranean cake is packed with the flavours of Sicily with its hillsides of olive, orange and lemon trees, almonds in baskets and bottles of orange flower water redolent of its Arab past. Instead of flour there is semolina and ground almonds; instead of butter, there is oil and there are no dairy products whatsoever. Serve dusted with icing sugar with a scoop of citrus sorbet. Alternatively, enjoy it purely as a cake with a tiny espresso and a glass of ice-cold water.

semolina citrus cake

Reserve a little of the shredded lemon and orange zest and put the remainder in a bowl with the olive oil, sugar, salt, orange and lemon juice and eggs. Whisk together with an electric mixer or balloon whisk until well mixed and smooth.

Sieve the semolina and baking powder into a second bowl and add the ground almonds. Fold the almond essence and orange flower water into the egg mixture. Pour all at once into the dry ingredients, fold together, but do not overmix. Spoon into the prepared tin and smooth the top.

Bake towards the top of a preheated oven at 160°C (325°F) Gas 3 for 40–45 minutes or until pale gold at the edges and firm in the middle. A skewer pushed into the centre should come out clean.

Remove from the oven and let cool in the tin for about 10 minutes. Drizzle the liqueur over the top. Push the cake out, still on its loose metal base, and let cool on a wire rack for another 10 minutes. Remove the base and peel off the paper. Serve in 8 or 12 wedges, warm or cool, but not chilled.

The cake will keep in an airtight container for up to 4 days.

shredded or grated zest and juice of 1 lemon

shredded or grated zest and juice of 1 orange

185 ml extra virgin olive oil

215 g caster sugar

¼ teaspoon salt

3 eggs

200 g semolina

115 g ground almonds

1 teaspoon baking powder

1 teaspoon almond essence

1 teaspoon orange flower water

4 tablespoons Cointreau or Grand Marnier

a loose-bottomed round cake tin, 23 cm diameter, lightly oiled and base-lined

SERVES 8–12

cinnamon toast with honey

150 ml milk

1 vanilla pod, split lengthways

freshly grated zest of 1 lemon

3 large eggs, beaten

1 long baguette-style loaf,
cut into 8 slices

60 ml moscatel wine

olive oil, for frying

TO SERVE

90 ml clear honey

ground cinnamon, for dusting

5 sugar cubes, coarsely crushed

SERVES 4–8

A more delicious version of French toast, torrija is one of Spain's best-loved treats. It is a sweet bread fritter that is eaten for dessert or in confiserías (cake shops) as a snack with a café cortado (coffee with a 'cut' of milk). Easter is the big time for torrijas, but you find them all year round. In Spain, you would use the everyday pan de pueblo – a long loaf with a crisp crust – but a baguette will work fine.

Put the milk in a saucepan with the vanilla pod and lemon zest and heat to just below boiling point. Remove from the heat and let cool. When cool, beat in the eggs.

Strain the mixture into a flat dish large enough to take 2 slices of bread at a time. Put the slices of bread on a tray and sprinkle with the wine, just to moisten slightly.

Dip 2 slices of bread into the egg mixture and let soak for a few minutes. Heat the olive oil in a frying pan over medium heat, add the soaked bread and fry until golden brown on both sides, about 4 minutes. Drain on kitchen paper. Repeat until all are done.

Transfer to a large serving dish and spoon over the honey, sprinkle with cinnamon and sugar and either let soak for a few hours or eat while hot.

If eating them cold, add the sugar just before serving.

a pinch of salt

finely grated zest of 1 lemon

1 teaspoon sunflower oil,
plus extra for deep-frying

140 g plain flour, sifted

1 large egg, beaten with
1 tablespoon cold water

caster sugar, for dusting

CHOCOLATE A LA TAZA

250 g plain dark chocolate,
about 50% cocoa solids, broken
into squares

2 tablespoons caster sugar

a stick of cinnamon

2 tablespoons fine rice flour

an electric deep-fryer (optional)

*a strong pastry bag fitted with
a star nozzle*

a wide, oiled spatula

MAKES ABOUT 12: SERVES 4

After a night of revelry doing what Spaniards do best (eating, drinking and talking), churros and hot chocolate at dawn are compulsory, ensuring a blissful sleep. A chocolate a la taza (cup of hot chocolate) for dunking churros must be thick – more like a sauce than a drink. The commercial chocolate made for this purpose has rice flour in it.

churros with hot chocolate

To make the churros, put 250 ml cold water in a medium saucepan with the salt, lemon zest and oil. Bring to a fast boil, then add the flour all at once. Beat quickly with a wooden spoon to bring the mixture to a smooth paste, then leave for 5 minutes. Beat the egg mixture into the paste a little at a time until smooth and thick.

Fill a saucepan or deep-fryer one-third full with the oil, or to the manufacturer's recommended level. Heat to 190°C (375°F).

Working in batches if necessary, spoon the mixture into the pastry bag. Pipe horseshoe shapes onto the oiled spatula, cutting the flow of dough at 15-cm intervals with a knife or scissors. Slide them into the oil and fry for about 4 minutes until a rich gold, drain on kitchen paper and dust with sugar, heaping it on top as well, in true Spanish style.

To make the *chocolate a la taza*, put the chocolate, sugar and 800 ml cold water in a saucepan with the cinnamon stick and slowly melt the chocolate. Put the rice flour in small bowl, add 4 tablespoons cold water and mix until smooth. Blend it into the chocolate, mix well and bring just to the boil. If too thick, add a little water and reheat. Serve hot with the churros.

iced lemon crush

coarsely grated zest and freshly squeezed
juice of 8 lemons

200 g caster sugar

crushed ice (optional)

SERVES 4

Put the zest and sugar in a saucepan with
250 ml cold water and bring to the boil for
5 minutes. Strain. Add 500 ml cold water
and the lemon juice, pour into a freezerproof
container and freeze for about 1 hour until ice
crystals have formed around the edge. Break
up with a fork and serve. Add extra crushed
ice, if using.

*Both of these drinks are perfect on baking hot days.
Iced lemon crush is just a very simple lemonade. The
Moorish version of horchata was made with pine nuts,
seeds and chufas or tiger nuts (which aren't nuts, but a
tuberous root) and used as a 'pick-me-up'. Almonds
can also be used instead of tiger nuts. The drink can
be found freshly made in horchaterias and ice cream
parlours, chilled and delicious.*

horchata

250 g blanched almonds, coarsely chopped

3 tablespoons sugar

freshly squeezed juice of 1 lemon

crushed ice, to serve (optional)

ground cinnamon, for dusting

SERVES 4

Put the almonds, sugar and 250 ml water in a blender and
grind as finely as possible. Pour into a jug or bowl and add
625 ml boiling water. Set aside to infuse for several hours until
completely cold. Strain through a fine-mesh nylon sieve into a
jug or bowl, pressing the liquid through with the back of a ladle.
Stir in the lemon juice and pour into a freezerproof container.

Freeze for about 1 hour until crystals start to form. Stir well and
serve in tall glasses with extra crushed ice, if using, and a
dusting of cinnamon.

Mint tea is very soothing after a spicy meal. The sugar is traditionally added before the boiling water, but you may wish to serve it separately. Don't use spearmint as it will taste like mouthwash.

moroccan mint tea

Heat the teapot with just-boiled water. Tip out the water, add the tea leaves and pour a little boiling water over them just to moisten. Swirl around, then quickly pour the water out again, taking care not to lose any leaves. Add a good handful of mint (add the sugar at this stage, if liked). Pour about 1 litre boiling water over the mint and moistened tea leaves. Put on the lid and leave to infuse for 5–8 minutes. Pour into warmed glasses and top with a few extra mint leaves. Hand the sugar around separately, if liked.

1½ heaped tablespoons green tea leaves

a handful of fresh mint leaves

about 150–180 g sugar, or to taste

SERVES 6

index

credits

RECIPES

Clare Ferguson
Babaghannouj
Bitter chocolate and
  hazelnut gelato
Boeuf en daube
Bouillabaisse
Bresaola and rocket with
  olive oil and Parmesan
Caponata
Chicken liver and bacon
Chicken tagine with
  apricots
Chickpea fritters
Clams with chilli parsley
  sauce
Classic lemon tart
Fougasse
Greek chicken stifado
Greek honey, walnut and
  brandy cake
Linguine with pesto alla
  genovese
Luganega country
  sausage with lentils and
  wilted greens
Moroccan-style
  marinated black olives
Pappardelle with seafood
  sauce
Peppers stuffed with
  caperberries
Piperrada
Pork fillet with Marsala
Provençal roasted
  chicken with garlic,
  lemons and olives
Provençal vegetable tian
Salade Niçoise
Sicilian schiacciata
Seafood with couscous
Semolina citrus cake
Sicilian spaghetti
Spaghetti alla carbonara
Spanish fishcakes
Spanish flans
Spanish roasted
  vegetables
Sugared strawberries

Linda Tubby
Artichokes provençal
Churros with hot chocolate
Cinnamon toast with
  honey
Cream of asparagus soup
Duck with olives
Garlic prawns
Gazpacho
Hake in garlic sauce with
  clams
Horchata
Iced lemon crush
Lamb cutlets with salsa
  salmoretta
Mint and parsley salad
Pan-grilled steaks with
  olive sauce
Potato fritters with chorizo
Salad of chicory leaves
  and blue cheese

Maxine Clark
Almond milk granita,
  laced with Amaretto
Braised sea bass with
  fennel and green olives
Caramelized fig tart
Cassoulet
Cauliflower with saffron
  and toasted
  breadcrumbs
Egyptian dukkah
Fresh tuna carpaccio
Grilled mixed vegetable
  salad with balsamic
  herb dressing
Grilled sardines with
  salmoriglio sauce
Meat roll simmered in
  tomato sauce
Moroccan butterflied and
  barbecued lamb
Moroccan mint tea
Moules marinière
Orange, escarole and
  black olive salad
Paella
Panna cotta with candied
  orange zest
Pissaladière
Pizza alla margherita
Pizza rustica
Pork and fennel
  meatballs in tomato
  sauce
Ratatouille
Red mullet and orange
  parcels
Rosemary focaccia
Sesame and mint
  couscous with winter
  vegetables
Sicilian green vegetables
Slow-roasted tomatoes
  on bruschetta with
  salted ricotta
Spinach with anchovies
  and pine nuts
Sweet and sour carrots
  and courgettes with mint
Three marinated antipasti
Tomato, mozzarella and
  basil salad
Vanilla gelato with hot
  cherry sauce
Watermelon sorbet with
  chocolate chip seeds
White bean and black
  olive crostini
Whole onions baked in
  their skins

Elsa Petersen-Schepelern
Avgolemono
French duck salade tiède
Greek salad
Neopolitan seafood stew
Soupe au pistou
Tonno e fagioli
Warm chicken salad with
  harissa dressing

Fran Warde
Osso bucco with
  gremolata
Warm Mediterranean
  Puy lentil salad

Rena Salaman
Baked aubergines with
  garlic and tomatoes
Baked kibbeh
Falafel
Grilled tuna kebabs
Hoummus
Okra with dried limes
Spicy meat pastries
Spinach and cheese pie
Stuffed vine leaves

Jennie Shapter
Char-grilled pepper
  frittata

Brian Glover
Fish baked with lemon,
  oregano and potatoes
Grilled fish with
  chermoula and grilled
  lemons

Silvana Franco
Pasta con le vongole

Louise Pickford
Souvlaki with bulghur
  wheat salad
Turkish pizza turnover

Sonia Stevenson
Roast gigot of monkfish
  with sauce Niçoise
Tuna with paprika crumbs
  and romesco sauce

PHOTOGRAPHS

Key: a=above, b=below,
r=right, l=left, c=centre

Peter Cassidy
Pages 1, 3 all, 4l, 4-5, 7,
8al, 8ac, 8br, 11, 12, 15,
16, 21, 28, 31, 35, 39,
40, 44, 48al, 48br, 49,
55, 56, 67, 73, 74, 79,
80, 82bl, 92, 95, 102,
106, 112ar, 112bl,
112br, 113, 114, 117,
130, 145, 146, 148al,
148bl, 148br, 149, 150,
159, 160, 165, 166,
168, 171, 172, 175,
176, 178al, 178bl,
178br, 183, 185, 204br,
224, 227

Martin Brigdale
Pages 5r, 22, 32, 37, 43,
48ar, 51, 52, 58, 63,
64, 77, 82br, 90, 97,
101, 105, 109, 119,
120, 123, 129, 135,
136, 139, 143, 156,
163, 178ac, 178ar,
180, 189, 190, 193,
197, 199, 200, 206,
209, 211, 212, 214, 221,
222, 228, 231, 232

Noel Murphy
Pages 19, 83, 84, 89,
124, 132, 153, 155,
179, 194, 235

Debi Treloar
Pages 8bl, 69, 82al,
140, 148ar, 204ar,
204bl

Jan Baldwin
Pages 8ar, 82al, 82bc,
endpapers

Ian Wallace
Pages 112al, 127, 202,
204al

Jean Cazals
Pages 205, 217, 219

Gus Filgate
Pages 9, 25, 26

Diana Miller
Pages 48bl, 61, 70

Richard Jung
Pages 98, 111

Chris Tubbs
Pages 2, 6

Tara Fisher
Page 47

Jeremy Hopley
Page 87

Tom Leighton
Page 204ac

William Lingwood
Page 186